Reigning
Cats & Dogs
The Pets That *Rule* Our Lives

Best Wishes!

Elliot Engel

Reigning
Cats & Dogs
The Pets That *Rule* Our Lives

DR. ELLIOT ENGEL

Denise Clark

Quinn Hawkesworth

This book is lovingly dedicated to:

Kit and Kaboodle
Hibou, Io, and Pippa
Carroty Bob, Cluny, and Harry Spotter
Rooney and Sissy Belle

Who are the greatest dogs and cats *EVER*–
except, of course, for yours!

"Our perfect companions never have fewer
than four feet." --- Colette

I have done mostly what most men do,
And pushed it out of my mind;
But I can't forget, if I wanted to,
Four-feet trotting behind.

Day after day, the whole day through,
Wherever my road inclined,
Four-feet said, "I am coming with you?"
And trotted along behind.

Now I must go by some other round,
Which I shall never find,
Somewhere that does not carry the sound
Of Four-feet trotting behind.

---Rudyard Kipling, "Four Feet"

I like pigs. Dogs look up to us. Cats look down on us. Pigs treat us as equal.
--- Winston Churchill

Table of Contents

Introduction

One of the reasons that literature has always been my passion is that all of life can be found within the pages of our greatest authors. As one of my favorite English professors once defined it: "Literature is the study of what it is to be a human being."

And, actually, literature is far broader than even that all-encompassing definition. As this book should prove, literature also can show us what it is like to be an animal; better yet, it can show us what it is like to be our *very* favorite animals – cats and dogs – who are, of course, to most of us really just family with fur.

We have selected our favorite short stories, ancient tales, and poems (alas, no doggerel) which deal with cats and dogs, and we have placed them in sixteen chapters: nine for cats to symbolize their many, many lives and seven for dogs to symbolize the seven-to-one ratio that makes their years zip by compared to us humans. We hope many of these tales and poems become new favorites for you, and that you therefore mark them for frequent return readings by "dog-earing" our book.

You'll note that each chapter begins with a short essay which I originally wrote for our Dickens Disciples or Authors Ink newsletters of many years ago. I waded through one hundred of them recently and selected sixteen of my favorites, and so I have labeled each a "Teacher's Pet" to be placed at the beginning of each chapter. Although these essays seemingly have little or nothing to do with cats or dogs, I do explain, without fetching too far, why they precede the literature in their particular chapters. I hope you enjoy them.

Our final section contains some dog-gone great recipes for you to try, a few of which are designed for pets only, and all are appropriately named after our canine and feline companions. The recipes are usually for generous portions to allow you at the end of the meal to reach for that marvelous twentieth-century restaurant invention: the doggie bag.

We ask for your forgiveness at this point in case we did not include a favorite pet story or poem of yours in these pages. As punishment we shall banish ourselves to the Doghouse which, when you think about it, might be lonely but is far more respectable and less stimulating than being banished to the Cathouse.

Above all, we hope our little volume brings to the forefront the enormous contributions that cats and dogs have given as pets to the happiness of the entire human race. Yes, yes, we have heard that our pets are the only member of our family who grant us the precious gift of unconditional love, but these tales of the tails that wag and twitch within this anthology celebrate also, in most cases, the unconditional love that we give right back to our devoted darlings.

Too often in literature pets are merely part of the background scenery in domestic novels, or thematic symbols of Fidelity or Aloofness in epic poetry. Not here. REIGNING CATS & DOGS puts these beloved creatures front and center in each chapter. Not surprisingly we turn to William Shakespeare to express most vividly this centrality of beloved pets. In the first scene of the last act of what is arguably the most famous work in all world literature – his immortal *Hamlet* – Shakespeare once and for all shines the spotlight directly on cats and dogs, even at the expense of the son of Jupiter. Hamlet says to Laertes:

"Let Hercules himself do what he may
The cat will mew and dog will have his day."

Indeed, we give the dog his day in this book, and although this volume may not achieve the ultimate compliment of being the cat's meow, we can tell you that as we searched and gathered the following delightful pieces, we took a journey through great literature in the enviable position of sitting high in the catbird seat.

Elliot Engel
Dog Days of August, 2010

Cat

Catling

Feline

Gatto

Gib

Kitten

Kitty

Molly

Moggie

Mouser

Puss

Pussy

Queen

Sire

Tabby

Tomcat

Tom

> *What better way to begin this cat section than by introducing you to Charles Dickens' pet cat who sat faithfully next to his master late into the night when Dickens was composing at his writing desk? This particular cat had the hilarious habit, when bored by Dickens' too lengthy stay at the desk, of extinguishing Dickens' candle with a flick of his paw, thus abruptly ending that night's writing session. My essay also summons up the image of Dickens at his writing desk but for a very different reason.*

Talk about pressure. In February of 1850, when he was writing his monthly installments of *David Copperfield*, Charles Dickens ran out of paper and went to a stationer's shop to buy some. Perhaps he chose this particular shop because it sold his novels in current monthly issues. There was a woman ahead of him in line; he overheard her request to the clerk behind the counter: "I would like to purchase Installment Eleven of Mr. Dickens' latest novel." "I'm sorry," the clerk replied, "but that one has not been published yet."

As Dickens wrote to his friend John Forster later that day, a shiver went down his spine when he realized that he was standing in line to buy paper to begin writing the very chapters that his public was already demanding. Here was an artist so physically close to his audience that they would stand in a line together with the same goal in mind: Chapters 31, 32, and 33 of *David Copperfield*!

But most critics agree that if Dickens had been writing in 2010 rather than 1850 he would not have been writing novels at all. He would probably have become a filmmaker, since movies have replaced the novel during the last hundred years as the artistic medium for those artists dedicated to reaching a mass audience. These critics point out that it has always been this way. William Shakespeare chose drama because it was the most exciting and accessible genre of the last decade of the 1500's; Byron, Keats, and Shelley chose poetry for the same reason in the first decade of the 1800's.

But movies today make Dickens' artistry as a novelist seem so personal and quaint in comparison. The last time I went to a movie, the scenery in the film was so spectacular that I stayed in my seat long after the final scene to watch the credits for the filming locations. Because that particular information came last, I was treated to the entire catalogue of those associated with the movie. I expected to see the production assistants, stunt performers, and costumers credited. I even expected to read the names of the "Best Boy" and "Key Grip," though I've never had the foggiest idea what possible job they perform. But I was startled when the catering company, the chauffeuring agency, and the Porta-toilet firm were also listed. I swear that there had to be over 400 names in those credits.

Compare that with Charles Dickens sitting at his desk in his study at home, inventing immortal characters and scenes which appeared on the page as fast as his quill could put them there, and then translating them to the entire reading public of the world with the assistance of a few printers and perhaps an editor or two. Is it any wonder that today we label his contributions as artistry and Steven Spielberg's contribution as show business?

I'm not implying that a Dickens novel by its genre alone is somehow more artistically satisfying or a greater work of art than David Selznick's *Gone With The Wind* or, for that matter, David Lean's classic film version of *Oliver Twist*. But it is true that Dickens had almost complete artistic control over his art, while movies today are not only a business but one in which hundreds of individuals contribute their unique talents.

Poor Dickens, of course, was not gaudily rewarded for his fictional efforts as filmmakers are today at the annual Academy Awards. Had there been such an organization back then for British novelists, can you imagine their anguish when they tried to pick a winner in the category of Best Novel of 1848 when the following four immortal works all first appeared: Thackeray's *Vanity Fair*, Charlotte Brontë's *Jane Eyre*, Dickens' *Dombey and Son*, and Emily Brontë's *Wuthering Heights*? This was truly an embarrassment of riches, whereas most of today's films are just true embarrassments.

It is significant to mention here that the word "author" has evolved as a shortened form of "authority." The magisterial authority Dickens commanded with the printed word can never be duplicated by a filmmaker in his or her movie. With a genius such as Dickens, a famous cliché is turned on its head, for in his case, a word is indeed worth a thousand pictures.

The Master's Cat
The Story of Charles Dickens as Told by His Cat

By Eleanor Poe Barlow

Charles Dickens lived a life as fascinating as that of any character he created. It was full of sadness and joy, poverty and wealth, mystery and fame.

As a sickly boy of twelve, Dickens was forced to work in a rat-ridden factory to earn money to free his family from a debtors' prison. By a twist of fate, he became a writer instead of an actor. He was the proud father of ten children, but he shocked England by separating from their mother. When he became famous, he lived at the centre of a glittering London circle of writers and artists; but in his last troubled years, he found peace in the quiet Gad's Hill circle of his family and friends. Gad's Hill Place was the country estate he brought in 1856, and it was there that he died in 1870.

In the last years Charles Dickens had a little four-footed companion, a deaf cat, who sat with him when he wrote and followed him wherever he went – around the house and on walks about his property and the countryside. Even worthier of note was this little creature's curious habit of putting out candles. We know about this loyal and clever cat because Dickens' children wrote about him: Mary, or Mamie as she was called, in her two books, *My Father as I Recall Him* and *Charles Dickens by His Eldest Daughter*, and Sir Henry Fielding Dickens in his book, *Memoirs of My Father*. Wherever the story can be told by Mamie or Sir Henry, I have let them do it.

I have chosen to introduce Charles Dickens to you through the eyes of his cat because his affection for the man should endear the author to you. He can tell you the great man's story filled with the daily doings and adventures of children and pets. He can also persuade his beloved master to go back in time and tell his own story.

Wherever possible I have given Charles Dickens his own words to speak. I have also given his words as found in letters, in his books, and in his autobiographical fragment to the cat in his descriptions of Gad's Hill, its family, its animals, and the habits of its master. This is to put you, my readers, as close as is possible to Charles Dickens. I have done this with the encouragement of Cedric Charles Dickens, great grandson of Charles Dickens and grandson of Sir Henry. Cedric set his family biographies before me at his home in Somerset, England, on a summer day in 1992. I had come fresh from two weeks of teaching at Gad's Hill School on a grant from the Dickens Fellowship.

Gad's Hill School? Yes, Charles Dickens' house is a school. It was there, amidst lessons and laughter, that this book was born. I walked the gardens and meadows where Dickens and his cat walked. I sat in the Study where Dickens wrote his last four books, his dear companion curled beside him. I felt close to them both and wanted to bring them back. For to know them would be to understand the generous, passionate, vulnerable nature of literature's great master and the devotion of that master's cat.

This is the story of my Master, Charles Dickens, the great English novelist. I tell it to you from some distant place, looking back in time to the years 1860 to 1870, the first ten years of my life and the last ten of my Master's. Where I could, I have used his words. For example, later in this Prologue I record my birth as David Copperfield recorded his. I learned the language literally at Mr. Dickens' elbow, for I was usually cuddled, front paws tucked under my chest, on his desk.

We lived at Gad's Hill Place, a lovely country house on the Dover Road, Higham-by-Rochester, Kent, England. My Master bought the house in 1856, when he was forty-four. It was for him the fulfillment of a childhood dream, but I will let him tell that story later.

Whether Dickens was in his Study or in his writing room across the road at this chalet, he was sure to have me as his companion. I belonged to him, and he belonged to me. He told me the story of his life in fragments as we sat together. I prompted them, I must admit, by a most unusual trick.

In the evening, when I grew tired of watching him read, or of seeing his pen scratch across one page of manuscript after another, I would simply stretch up on all fours, and with a quick dab of my paw extinguish the candle flame by which he read or wrote. A bemused smile would creep from the corners of his kindly eyes as he laid down his book or pen, and settled in his chair to travel back with me through the story of his life.

There is one last and most unusual thing for you to know. I relate it matter-of-factly, as most miracles are explained. I was born deaf, but I did not hold it as a disadvantage, for the simple reason that although I could not hear the songs of birds or crickets or the voice of my own dear mother, quite miraculously I could hear the voice of my Master and the voices of his youngest and dearest sons, Harry and Plorn. My Master's voice was always kindly, so full of drama as he told the most wonderful stories. But to get to these stories I must first tell my own.

To begin my life with the beginning of my life, I record that I was born (as I have been informed and believe) on a Friday, at twelve o'clock at night. My mother, a most beautiful cat named Williamina, was lying in a soft curl of blanket near the stove. Although she had a wish to be upstairs amidst the warmth and brightness of the family life, the Master of the house said her place was to be in the basement kitchen. So it was there that she gave birth to her little family at the midnight hour of 9 June, 1860.

My sisters and brothers and I numbered five. We were of various colours: one, all white like my mother; another, marbled brown and white; two, equal parts black and white; and one, me, a brown tabby (I prefer "tiger") with large green eyes over which, in perfect symmetry, peaked twin black lines, thus lending me a look of perpetual curiosity, which I can assure you I had.

My mother was a gentle but determined soul. She found favour with everyone in the house, but she was particularly devoted to the Master. She loved his company. For that reason, she had a fancy that her little family should live in the Study where the Master spent a good portion of his day alone, writing. So when we were still tiny kittens, she brought us upstairs, one by one, from the kitchen floor, and deposited us in a corner of the Study. We were promptly taken back downstairs by order of the Master, who said he could really not allow us to be in his room: he was far too busy to be distracted by kittens at play. My mother tried again, with the same result. But she was not to be defeated even by a Study door, now closed fast against us. On the third trip she carried me up the stairs, but this time she continued through the hall, out through the front door, and from the geranium bed to the Study window, jumped in with me in her mouth, and laid me down at the Master's feet. She made four more trips until the whole family was at last before him. She herself sat down beside us and gave an imploring look. Kindly man that he was, he could resist no longer, and Williamina carried the day.

As we grew, we became very rampageous and swarmed up the curtains and played on the writing table, and scampered among the bookshelves, and made such a noise as was never heard in the Study before. We took particular pleasure in looking at ourselves in the long mirrors on either side of the bay window, and in batting the feathers of the goose quill pens as we skittered them from desk to carpet.

On that desk we also found to our delight the bronze figures of two plump toads dueling, a small monkey in a pill-box hat, a statue of a dog-fancier with dogs under his arms and puppies peering out of his pockets, a gilt leaf with a rabbit sitting erect upon it, a little box of string, a paper knife and an inkstand of blue ink. To our credit we knew enough to tiptoe among these treasures, for they were Dickens's silent companions when he wrote, there for his eyes to rest upon as he spun his plots in his head.

We pretended to read the book titles, especially those painted to look like volumes on the back of the door to the hallway. No wonder, for I later learned that one of the sets of dummy bookbacks invented and labeled by the Master bore the title *Cats' Lives* and was in nine volumes!

Our mother knew when to settle us quietly in our corner near the fireplace. The same spirit that influenced the whole house must have been brought to bear upon us when the Master was writing, for we were never complained of, and we were never turned out of our home in the Study until the time came for finding other good homes for us.

"We will keep the little tabby," decreed the Master of the house. "He is exceptional and so must be accepted as a member of the family." He considered me singular, for in my deafness I preferred to scramble up onto his desk to keep him company while my sisters and brothers frolicked. Because I could not hear to come when summoned, I was given no name. But in consequence of my devotion to the Master of Gad's Hill, Charles Dickens, I was called The Master's Cat.

You have just read the prologue of Eleanor Poe Barlow's utterly delightful book, *The Master's Cat*. This twelve-chapter book is full of fascinating biographical information on Dickens and is told as only his favorite pet could do so. Should you wish to purchase an autographed copy of this book, contact Denise at 1-800-392-4434 or denise@AuthorsInk.com for details.

What greater gift than the love of a cat? --- Charles Dickens

You'll see that my essay, in a roundabout way, glorifies the lost virtues of slowness and pauses. Then when you read Kipling's tale, note how he too glories in leisureliness as he moves from man to dog to horse to cow most methodically as he convinces us why the Cat must Walk by Himself.

When I was a child I never spent one minute with my father in his workshop. There was no workshop. A complete inventory of the tools in the Engel household: one screwdriver, one hammer, and one wrench – all kept in the depths of the kitchen catch-all drawer. But I do vividly remember many times when I was dazzled by my father's manual dexterity. His instrument was neither a lathe nor a drill; it was a typewriter.

My father was an accomplished hunter-and-pecker who combined impressive speed, rhythm and accuracy. And so at a tender age of seven, watching him, I fell in love with everything connected with typing. I'm one of the few children who did not beg for a new model bicycle each birthday but instead always pleaded for an upgrade of my current typewriter.

I was enthralled the first time Dad boosted me up into his typing chair. I was so little that he needed to place the Indianapolis phone book beneath me (had we lived in a less-populated city, I never could have reached the keyboard.) When I first put my tiny fingers on the middle-row eight keys, I assumed they would be resting on A-B-C-D-E-F-G-H, the same alphabetical order I had recently memorized and proudly recited hourly until my sister threatened to shut me up.

I tapped the "A" and it appeared, like magic, shining blackly against the white sheet of paper. But when I tapped what I thought would be "B," an "S" appeared. When I looked down at the keys, there were A-S-D-F-J-K-L-; where A though H should have been.

I immediately asked my father what was probably my fiftieth question of that early Sunday morning: "Daddy, why did they put the letters in that order?" This time, for a change, it was a question worth asking. I still remember my father looking at the keys, thinking with furled brow, pausing, and then confessing: "Elliot, I don't know." There was another pause and then – "But I'll find out."

Of all the good examples my father bequeathed to me, the one I've probably appreciated the most as a teacher was his inability to give a facile guess to a question he could not answer. He always made it his mission to answer with accuracy, and I owe him an enormous debt for inspiring a love of research in me. He called the reference librarian at our downtown branch who told him she would have to do some checking and call him back. Imagine my glee in posing a question that not only stumped my brilliant father but even puzzled the "Reference Librarian," an august title which, to a seven-year-old, sounded like Merriam Webster himself.

She did call right back. Although I didn't fully understand his explanation to me at the time. Dad told me that the original typewriter designer worried about key jamming that would occur if the letter that had just struck the paper did not have enough time to fall back before the next one arrived. And so the designer intentionally placed the letters on the keyboard in a difficult, illogical pattern to frustrate and slow the typist down to the capabilities of the machine. This slowing ironically made the process of typing more efficient.

I feel that there's a lesson here about the Virtue of Slow as we now speed in the computer age of Instant Information and Gratification, while the typewriter will be joining the record player and slide rule on the shelves of future antique stores. The act of reading a book is so much slower than watching a film or television show. Yet the demands made on us by following a narrative word by word by word often make the ultimate experience profoundly more rewarding. Similarly, with all the good answers my father patiently gave me during my childhood, it is his pauses that most impress me now, as he carefully thought about his responses, indicating not only a respect for the question but, even better, a respect for the questioner, his young son who adored him.

The Cat That Walked By Himself

By Rudyard Kipling

HEAR and attend and listen; for this befell and behappened and became and was, O my Best Beloved, when the Tame animals were wild. The Dog was wild, and the Horse was wild, and the Cow was wild, and the Sheep was wild, and the Pig was wild—as wild as wild could be—and they walked in the Wet Wild Woods by their wild lones. But the wildest of all the wild animals was the Cat. He walked by himself, and all places were alike to him.

Of course the Man was wild too. He was dreadfully wild. He didn't even begin to be tame till he met the Woman, and she told him that she did not like living in his wild ways. She picked out a nice dry Cave, instead of a heap of wet leaves, to lie down in; and she strewed clean sand on the floor; and she lit a nice fire of wood at the back of the Cave; and she hung a dried wild-horse skin, tail-down, across the opening of the Cave; and she said, 'Wipe your feet, dear, when you come in, and now we'll keep house.'

That night, Best Beloved, they ate wild sheep roasted on the hot stones, and flavoured with wild garlic and wild pepper; and wild duck stuffed with wild rice and wild fenugreek and wild coriander; and marrow-bones of wild oxen; and wild cherries, and wild grenadillas. Then the Man went to sleep in front of the fire ever so happy; but the Woman sat up, combing her hair. She took the bone of the shoulder of mutton—the big fat blade-bone—and she looked at the wonderful marks on it, and she threw more wood on the fire, and she made a Magic. She made the First Singing Magic in the world.

Out in the Wet Wild Woods all the wild animals gathered together where they could see the light of the fire a long way off, and they wondered what it meant.

Then Wild Horse stamped with his wild foot and said, 'O my Friends and O my Enemies, why have the Man and the

11

Woman made that great light in that great Cave, and what harm will it do us?'

Wild Dog lifted up his wild nose and smelled the smell of roast mutton, and said, 'I will go up and see and look, and say; for I think it is good. Cat, come with me.'

'Nenni!' said the Cat. 'I am the Cat who walks by himself, and all places are alike to me. I will not come.'

'Then we can never be friends again,' said Wild Dog, and he trotted off to the Cave. But when he had gone a little way the Cat said to himself, 'All places are alike to me. Why should I not go too and see and look and come away at my own liking.' So he slipped after Wild Dog softly, very softly, and hid himself where he could hear everything.

When Wild Dog reached the mouth of the Cave he lifted up the dried horse-skin with his nose and sniffed the beautiful smell of the roast mutton, and the Woman, looking at the blade-bone, heard him, and laughed, and said, 'Here comes the first. Wild Thing out of the Wild Woods, what do you want?'

Wild Dog said, 'O my Enemy and Wife of my Enemy, what is this that smells so good in the Wild Woods?'

Then the Woman picked up a roasted mutton-bone and threw it to Wild Dog, and said, 'Wild Thing out of the Wild Woods, taste and try.' Wild Dog gnawed the bone, and it was more delicious than anything he had ever tasted, and he said, 'O my Enemy and Wife of my Enemy, give me another.'

The Woman said, 'Wild Thing out of the Wild Woods, help my Man to hunt through the day and guard this Cave at night, and I will give you as many roast bones as you need.'

'Ah!' said the Cat, listening. 'This is a very wise Woman, but she is not so wise as I am.'

Wild Dog crawled into the Cave and laid his head on the Woman's lap, and said, 'O my Friend and Wife of my Friend, I will help Your Man to hunt through the day, and at night I will guard your Cave.'

'Ah!' said the Cat, listening. 'That is a very foolish Dog.' And he went back through the Wet Wild Woods waving his wild tail, and walking by his wild lone. But he never told anybody.

When the Man woke up he said, 'What is Wild Dog doing here?' And the Woman said, 'His name is not Wild Dog any more, but the First Friend, because he will be our friend for always and always and always. Take him with you when you go hunting.'

Next night the Woman cut great green armfuls of fresh grass from the water-meadows, and dried it before the fire, so that it smelt like new-mown hay, and she sat at the mouth of the Cave and plaited a halter out of horsehide, and she looked at the shoulder of mutton-bone—at the big broad blade-bone—and she made a Magic. She made the Second Singing Magic in the world.

Out in the Wild Woods all the wild animals wondered what had happened to Wild Dog, and at last Wild Horse stamped with his foot and said, 'I will go and see and say why Wild Dog has not returned. Cat, come with me.'

'Nenni!' said the Cat. 'I am the Cat who walks by himself, and all places are alike to me. I will not come.' But all the same he followed Wild Horse softly, very softly, and hid himself where he could hear everything.

When the Woman heard Wild Horse tripping and stumbling on his long mane, she laughed and said, 'Here comes the second. Wild Thing out of the Wild Woods what do you want?'

Wild Horse said, 'O my Enemy and Wife of my Enemy, where is Wild Dog?'

The Woman laughed, and picked up the blade-bone and looked at it, and said, 'Wild Thing out of the Wild Woods, you did not come here for Wild Dog, but for the sake of this good grass.'

And Wild Horse, tripping and stumbling on his long mane, said, 'That is true; give it to me to eat.'

The Woman said, 'Wild Thing out of the Wild Woods, bend your wild head and wear what I give you, and you shall eat the wonderful grass three times a day.'

'Ah,' said the Cat, listening, 'this is a clever Woman, but she is not so clever as I am.' Wild Horse bent his wild head, and the Woman slipped the plaited hide halter over it, and Wild Horse breathed on the Woman's feet and said, 'O my Mistress, and Wife of my Master, I will be your servant for the sake of the wonderful grass.'

'Ah,' said the Cat, listening, 'that is a very foolish Horse.' And he went back through the Wet Wild Woods, waving his wild tail and walking by his wild lone. But he never told anybody.

When the Man and the Dog came back from hunting, the Man said, 'What is Wild Horse doing here?' And the Woman said, 'His name is not Wild Horse any more, but the First Servant, because he will carry us from place to place for always and always and always. Ride on his back when you go hunting.

Next day, holding her wild head high that her wild horns should not catch in the wild trees, Wild Cow came up to the Cave, and the Cat followed, and hid himself just the same as before; and everything happened just the same as before; and the Cat said the same things as before, and when Wild Cow had promised to give her milk to the Woman every day in exchange for the wonderful grass, the Cat went back through the Wet Wild Woods waving his wild tail and walking by his wild lone, just the same as before. But he never told anybody. And when the Man and the Horse and the Dog came home from hunting and asked the same questions same as before, the Woman said, 'Her name is not Wild Cow any more, but the Giver of Good Food. She will give us the warm white milk for always and always and always, and I will take care of her while you and the First Friend and the First Servant go hunting.

Next day the Cat waited to see if any other Wild thing would go up to the Cave, but no one moved in the Wet Wild Woods, so the Cat walked there by himself; and he saw the Woman milking the Cow, and he saw the light of the fire in the Cave, and he smelt the smell of the warm white milk.

Cat said, 'O my Enemy and Wife of my Enemy, where did Wild Cow go?'

The Woman laughed and said, 'Wild Thing out of the Wild Woods, go back to the Woods again, for I have braided up my hair, and I have put away the magic blade-bone, and we have no more need of either friends or servants in our Cave.

Cat said, 'I am not a friend, and I am not a servant. I am the Cat who walks by himself, and I wish to come into your cave.'

Woman said, 'Then why did you not come with First Friend on the first night?'

Cat grew very angry and said, 'Has Wild Dog told tales of me?'

Then the Woman laughed and said, 'You are the Cat who walks by himself, and all places are alike to you. You are neither a friend nor a servant. You have said it yourself. Go away and walk by yourself in all places alike.'

Then Cat pretended to be sorry and said, 'Must I never come into the Cave? Must I never sit by the warm fire? Must I never drink the warm white milk? You are very wise and very beautiful. You should not be cruel even to a Cat.'

Woman said, 'I knew I was wise, but I did not know I was beautiful. So I will make a bargain with you. If ever I say one word in your praise you may come into the Cave.'

'And if you say two words in my praise?' said the Cat.

'I never shall,' said the Woman, 'but if I say two words in your praise, you may sit by the fire in the Cave.'

'And if you say three words?' said the Cat.

'I never shall,' said the Woman, 'but if I say three words in your praise, you may drink the warm white milk three times a day for always and always and always.'

Then the Cat arched his back and said, 'Now let the Curtain at the mouth of the Cave, and the Fire at the back of the Cave, and the Milk-pots that stand beside the Fire, remember what my Enemy and the Wife of my Enemy has said.' And he went away through the Wet Wild Woods waving his wild tail and walking by his wild lone.

That night when the Man and the Horse and the Dog came home from hunting, the Woman did not tell them of the bargain that she had made with the Cat, because she was afraid that they might not like it.

Cat went far and far away and hid himself in the Wet Wild Woods by his wild lone for a long time till the Woman forgot all about him. Only the Bat—the little upside-down Bat—that hung inside the Cave, knew where Cat hid; and every evening Bat would fly to Cat with news of what was happening.

One evening Bat said, 'There is a Baby in the Cave. He is new and pink and fat and small, and the Woman is very fond of him.'

'Ah,' said the Cat, listening, 'but what is the Baby fond of?'

'He is fond of things that are soft and tickle,' said the Bat. 'He is fond of warm things to hold in his arms when he goes to sleep. He is fond of being played with. He is fond of all those things.'

'Ah,' said the Cat, listening, 'then my time has come.'

Next night Cat walked through the Wet Wild Woods and hid very near the Cave till morning-time, and Man and Dog and Horse went hunting. The Woman was busy cooking that morning, and the Baby cried and interrupted. So she carried him outside the Cave and gave him a handful of pebbles to play with. But still the Baby cried.

Then the Cat put out his paddy paw and patted the Baby on the cheek, and it cooed; and the Cat rubbed against its fat knees and tickled it under its fat chin with his tail. And the Baby laughed; and the Woman heard him and smiled.

Then the Bat—the little upside-down Bat—that hung in the mouth of the Cave said, 'O my Hostess and Wife of my Host and Mother of my Host's Son, a Wild Thing from the Wild Woods is most beautifully playing with your Baby.'

'A blessing on that Wild Thing whoever he may be,' said the Woman, straightening her back, 'for I was a busy woman this morning and he has done me a service.'

That very minute and second, Best Beloved, the dried horse-skin Curtain that was stretched tail-down at the mouth of the Cave fell down—whoosh!—because it remembered the bargain she had made with the Cat, and when the Woman went to pick it up—lo and behold!—the Cat was sitting quite comfy inside the Cave.

'O my Enemy and Wife of my Enemy and Mother of my Enemy,' said the Cat, 'it is I: for you have spoken a word in my praise, and now I can sit within the Cave for always and always and always. But still I am the Cat who walks by himself, and all places are alike to me.'

The Woman was very angry, and shut her lips tight and took up her spinning-whorl and began to spin. But the Baby cried because the Cat had gone away, and the Woman could not hush it, for it struggled and kicked and grew black in the face.

'O my Enemy and Wife of my Enemy and Mother of my Enemy,' said the Cat, 'take a strand of the wire that you are spinning and tie it to your spinning-whorl and drag it along the floor, and I will show you a magic that shall make your Baby laugh as loudly as he is now crying.'

16

'I will do so,' said the Woman, 'because I am at my wits' end; but I will not thank you for it.'

She tied the thread to the little clay spindle whorl and drew it across the floor, and the Cat ran after it and patted it with his paws and rolled head over heels, and tossed it backward over his shoulder and chased it between his hind-legs and pretended to lose it, and pounced down upon it again, till the Baby laughed as loudly as it had been crying, and scrambled after the Cat and frolicked all over the Cave till it grew tired and settled down to sleep with the Cat in its arms.

'Now,' said the Cat, 'I will sing the Baby a song that shall keep him asleep for an hour. And he began to purr, loud and low, low and loud, till the Baby fell fast asleep. The Woman smiled as she looked down upon the two of them and said, 'That was wonderfully done. No question but you are very clever, O Cat.'

That very minute and second, Best Beloved, the smoke of the fire at the back of the Cave came down in clouds from the roof—puff!—because it remembered the bargain she had made with the Cat, and when it had cleared away—lo and behold— the Cat was sitting quite comfy close to the fire.

'O my Enemy and Wife of my Enemy and Mother of My Enemy,' said the Cat, 'it is I, for you have spoken a second word in my praise, and now I can sit by the warm fire at the back of the Cave for always and always and always. But still I am the Cat who walks by himself, and all places are alike to me.'

Then the Woman was very very angry, and let down her hair and put more wood on the fire and brought out the broad blade-bone of the shoulder of mutton and began to make a Magic that should prevent her from saying a third word in praise of the Cat. It was not a Singing Magic, Best Beloved, it was a Still Magic; and by and by the Cave grew so still that a little wee-wee mouse crept out of a corner and ran across the floor.

'O my Enemy and Wife of my Enemy and Mother of my Enemy,' said the Cat, 'is that little mouse part of your magic?'

'Ouh! Chee! No indeed!' said the Woman, and she dropped the blade-bone and jumped upon the footstool in front of the fire and braided up her hair very quick for fear that the mouse should run up it.

'Ah,' said the Cat, watching, 'then the mouse will do me no harm if I eat it?'

'No,' said the Woman, braiding up her hair, 'eat it quickly and I will ever be grateful to you.'

Cat made one jump and caught the little mouse, and the Woman said, 'A hundred thanks. Even the First Friend is not quick enough to catch little mice as you have done. You must be very wise.'

That very moment and second, O Best Beloved, the Milk-pot that stood by the fire cracked in two pieces—ffft—because it remembered the bargain she had made with the Cat, and when the Woman jumped down from the footstool—lo and behold!—the Cat was lapping up the warm white milk that lay in one of the broken pieces.

'O my Enemy and Wife of my Enemy and Mother of my Enemy, said the Cat, 'it is I; for you have spoken three words in my praise, and now I can drink the warm white milk three times a day for always and always and always. But still I am the Cat who walks by himself, and all places are alike to me.'

Then the Woman laughed and set the Cat a bowl of the warm white milk and said, 'O Cat, you are as clever as a man, but remember that your bargain was not made with the Man or the Dog, and I do not know what they will do when they come home.'

'What is that to me?' said the Cat. 'If I have my place in the Cave by the fire and my warm white milk three times a day I do not care what the Man or the Dog can do.'

That evening when the Man and the Dog came into the Cave, the Woman told them all the story of the bargain while the Cat sat by the fire and smiled. Then the Man said, 'Yes, but he has not made a bargain with me or with all proper Men after me.' Then he took off his two leather boots and he took up his little stone axe (that makes three) and he fetched a piece of wood and a hatchet (that is five altogether), and he set them out in a row and he said, 'Now we will make our bargain. If you do not catch mice when you are in the Cave for always and always and always, I will throw these five things at you whenever I see you, and so shall all proper Men do after me.'

'Ah,' said the Woman, listening, 'this is a very clever Cat, but he is not so clever as my Man.'

The Cat counted the five things (and they looked very knobby) and he said, 'I will catch mice when I am in the Cave for always and always and always; but still I am the Cat who walks by himself, and all places are alike to me.'

'Not when I am near,' said the Man. 'If you had not said that last I would have put all these things away for always and always and always; but I am now going to throw my two boots and my little stone axe (that makes three) at you whenever I meet you. And so shall all proper Men do after me!'

Then the Dog said, 'Wait a minute. He has not made a bargain with me or with all proper Dogs after me.' And he showed his teeth and said, 'If you are not kind to the Baby while I am in the Cave for always and always and always, I will hunt you till I catch you, and when I catch you I will bite you. And so shall all proper Dogs do after me.'

'Ah,' said the Woman, listening, 'this is a very clever Cat, but he is not so clever as the Dog.'

Cat counted the Dog's teeth (and they looked very pointed) and he said, 'I will be kind to the Baby while I am in the Cave, as long as he does not pull my tail too hard, for always and always and always. But still I am the Cat that walks by himself, and all places are alike to me.'

'Not when I am near,' said the Dog. 'If you had not said that last I would have shut my mouth for always and always and always; but now I am going to hunt you up a tree whenever I meet you. And so shall all proper Dogs do after me.'

Then the Man threw his two boots and his little stone axe (that makes three) at the Cat, and the Cat ran out of the Cave and the Dog chased him up a tree; and from that day to this, Best Beloved, three proper Men out of five will always throw things at a Cat whenever they meet him, and all proper Dogs will chase him up a tree. But the Cat keeps his side of the bargain too. He will kill mice and he will be kind to Babies when he is in the house, just as long as they do not pull his tail too hard. But when he has done that, and between times, and when the moon gets up and night comes, he is the Cat that walks by himself, and all places are alike to him. Then he goes out to the Wet Wild Woods or up the Wet Wild Trees or on the Wet Wild Roofs, waving his wild tail and walking by his wild lone.

19

PUSSY can sit by the fire and sing,
Pussy can climb a tree,
Or play with a silly old cork and string
To'muse herself, not me.
But I like Binkie my dog, because
He Knows how to behave;
So, Binkie's the same as the First Friend was,
And I am the Man in the Cave.

Pussy will play man-Friday till
It's time to wet her paw
And make her walk on the window-sill
(For the footprint Crusoe saw);
Then she fluffles her tail and mews,
And scratches and won't attend.
But Binkie will play whatever I choose,
And he is my true First Friend.

Pussy will rub my knees with her head
Pretending she loves me hard;
But the very minute I go to my bed
Pussy runs out in the yard,
And there she stays till the morning-light;
So I know it is only pretend;
But Binkie, he snores at my feet all night,
And he is my Firstest Friend!

> *Obviously, the theme that my essay and this traditional British fairy tale share is that of the Beautiful Princess. If only Diana had found a Prince Charming as worthy of her love as the other princess who spun herself into a frenzy to save her beloved.*

Although Princess Diana died back in 1997, you may remember that as the thousands of bouquets began covering the grounds of Kensington Palace, many newscasters said that there had never been such an overwhelming expression of love and grief at the death of a British dignitary – not for Churchill, not for the Duke of Wellington, not even for Queen Victoria. But they overlooked one: Charles Dickens. When Dickens died suddenly and most unexpectedly on June 9, 1870, at the age of fifty eight, not only was the public outpouring similar to that for Diana but the expression of it was, indeed, floral. Dickens was buried in Westminster Abbey, and the grave remained open until thousands of mourners passed; by the time the grave was closed the flowers overflowed into the Abbey.

But the flowers are not the connection to Diana that I find so extraordinary. Their chaotic lives contained eerie similarities, especially concerning the marital scandal that occupied the last decade of each. As with Diana, Dickens not only had a disastrous marriage but one that disintegrated in a most public manner, due to an astonishing decision made by Dickens himself. You remember that Diana decided to make her marital woes public by not only allowing but even contributing to the book by Andrew Morton (***Diana, Her True Story***) which graphically revealed the problems within her marriage to Prince Charles.

I doubt Diana was aware that 120 years earlier Charles Dickens, an equally irresistible celebrity to the masses, initiated the same strategy for garnering public sympathy and support. Believe it or not, when Dickens separated from Catherine in 1857, he took the extraordinarily risky step of publishing in his own magazine a first-hand account of the reasons he felt it necessary to dissolve the marriage. In print he accused his wife of being a bad mother and psychologically unsound (both baseless charges, by the way). And as with Diana the gamble paid off. His popularity never waned during this sordid episode. Regardless of the extramarital affairs they were alleged to have, both Diana and Dickens counted as their most cherished and important love affair the one they meticulously maintained with their public.

And isn't it more than coincidental that both of them performed public penance for their failings with the same type of good works? I cannot think of two other British subjects who more vividly symbolize in the public's mind the cause of sick children and the underprivileged in general than Charles Dickens and Princess Diana. And perhaps the sad motivation for these noble deeds is the same. The moving words that Diana's brother spoke at her funeral would have been equally appropriate 127 years earlier in the same Abbey where Dickens was eulogized: "For all the status, the fame, and applause, she remained throughout a very insecure person, at heart, almost childlike in her desire to do good for others so she could be released from deep feelings of unworthiness."

Less than two hours before Dickens was felled by a fatal stroke, he had written a letter in which he quoted Friar Laurence in *Romeo and Juliet*: "These violent delights have violent ends." In many ways, Shakespeare's words serve as a poignant epitaph for the dazzling yet self-destructive lives of Diana, Princess of Wales and Dickens, king of the English novel.

How Cats Got Their Purr

Traditional British Fairy Tale

There once lived a king and queen who longed for a baby daughter. Finally, just as they were giving up hope, the queen bore a girl child and the king and queen were the happiest people on earth. Only one thing marred their contentment. A gypsy witch had read the queen's fortune in return for some food from the royal kitchen and she had predicted that the child would be a girl. The gypsy had given the queen a dire warning and in anger the king had driven the old crone from his land. The old woman's warning weighed heavily on their hearts.

The old witch had said: "You will bear a daughter and she will be strong and healthy. However, she will fall dead if she ever gives her hand in marriage to a prince. Heed my advice. Find three pure white cats, with not a single white hair upon them, and let them grow up with your child. Give the cats balls of two types to play with - balls of gold and balls of linen thread. If they ignore the gold and play with the linen, all will be well, but should they ignore the linen and choose the gold, beware!"

The king sent out a royal decree and his subjects offered him cats and kittens of all types - tabby cats, ginger tomcats, tortoiseshell mother cats still nursing their kittens; he was offered black kittens, grey kittens and ginger kittens. All of these he sent away again, being only interested in three pure cats. After years of searching, three white cats without a single white hair were duly found and though they came from different places, they became good friends. The three cats loved their young mistress and she adored them. As the months turned into years, the linen balls continued to be the only toys the cats chose to play with. The gold balls lay dusty and forgotten.

When the princess grew old enough to learn how to spin the cats were happy as she was. They leaped at the wheel as it turned and at the thread as the princess spun it, behaving like kittens. She begged her playful cats to leave things alone but they ignored her and continued to play gaily. The queen was so happy that the cats played only with the linen balls and never with the gold balls that she simply laughed at their antics and frolics.

At sixteen years old, the princess was very beautiful. Princes from neighbouring kingdoms and further afield asked her hand in marriage, but she remained indifferent to them all. She was content to live with her three beloved cats. One day, however, a prince arrived who was good and charming, wise and handsome, kind and virtuous and the princess fell deeply in love with him. Though he brought her gifts and visited often, he never once asked for her hand in marriage. One day she could bear it no longer and she confessed her love for him. Delighted and surprise, he expressed his own love for her.

The three white cats were in the tower room playing with the linen balls, but no sooner had the prince and princess professed their love for each other, than the cats seemed to notice the gold balls for the first time ever and began to play with them. In horror, servants reported the dire news to the king and queen. However, it wasn't the princess who was struck down but the prince. He became gravely ill and nothing the physicians did could ease or cure whatever malady had struck him down.

In desperation the princess sought the gypsy who had made the prophecy about the cats and balls. The gypsy witch told her that there was only one way to save the prince. The princess must spin ten thousand skeins of pure white linen thread before midwinter's day. It was an impossible task - only 27 days remained before midwinter's day. No hand but hers could spin the thread and if she span but one skein too few, or one too many, the prince would die at midwinter. The princess rushed to her spinning wheel and worked steadily day after day, but after only a few days she knew she could never spin ten thousand skeins. She burst into tears and her three cats sat by her feet to comfort and console her.

"If you only knew what was wrong I know you'd help me if you could," she said to the three silent white cats at her feet.

To her amazement, one of the three placed its front paws on her knee, stared into the princess's face, opened its mouth and spoke to her: "We know what is needed and we know how to help you," it said. "Cats have no hands, only paws, so we can do the spinning for you and it will not break the terms of the prophecy. Now we must get to work for there is little time left."

And so it was that the three white cats began to spin, each at a wheel provided for it. Each spun rapidly and beautifully. All day the three wheels hummed and when they were silent as evening came the princess looked into the room to find her beloved cats sound asleep next to hundreds of skeins of thread. The days passed and the skeins increased in number. Each time a skein was finished, the prince's health improved and the princess grew more hopeful. On midwinter's eve ten thousand skeins were ready and the prince was almost well.

The gypsy was amazed and pleased at the cats' work though she had been cheated of a life. She told the princess to be sure and show her gratitude to her faithful cats. The princess loved her cats well and wisely and she gave them all her glittering jewels, which they had always loved to play with. On her wedding day, they sat in places of honour on magnificent velvet cushions, each cat with a necklace of precious stones around its neck.

As the feast continued, the three cats curled up contentedly on their cushions and—as cats are wont to do—fell asleep. From all three came loud, contented purring. This was the reward the cats had received for their work. Though no cat would ever again speak, all cats would purr like the whirr and hum of a spinning wheel. From that day to this day cats have continued to purr whenever they feel contented.

We live in an age of planned obsolescence in which what is oldest is almost never what is best. But in literature, I argue, the opposite is true. The historically oldest piece in our anthology – this story of "Dick Whittington and His Cat" —is from the 1300s and proves again that some of the finest creative writing was written in those times which stretch back furthest from ours.

Whenever I would read a novel which contained the rather stereotyped character of the Rich Uncle, I usually found him true to life, at least to mine. My rich uncle was a physician in a small northern Indiana town who had made his fortune in his very successful practice there. My most vivid memory of the numerous visits that my family made to his home was in the late 1950's when color televisions had just begun to be sold to the public. Since Uncle Max always had the first and best of everything, we were invited to spend an evening watching this remarkable invention.

It was a Sunday evening, and the program was *Dinah Shore's Variety Show* sponsored by Chevrolet. We all sat in my uncle's plush den marveling aloud at the incredible colors, while politely keeping to ourselves the fact that Dinah's face had never been that particular shade of orange nor had her hair ever glowed with the strange hue of a Christmas tree.

When my parents purchased our first color set a few years later I was amazed that not only was the color greatly improved but the price was significantly less than what Uncle Max said he had originally paid for his. This was the beginning of a phenomenon that has now become law in our computerized age: the first is never the best nor the least expensive. How many times in recent years have consumers rushed to take advantage of the initial sale of some computer or appliance, only to discover to their dismay that, had they waited another year, they could have possessed a finer and less expensive model?

It is no wonder that young people find it difficult to respect age, tradition, and elders in general when obsolescence now seems to be as absolute a law of nature as gravity. Is there any field left in which the most ancient is still the best? Indeed, there is: literature.

I shall never forget the fall semester of my senior year in college when I enrolled in three literature classes: History of Drama, Chaucer, and A Survey of the Novel. During the first week I was assigned the following work in each class: *Oedipus Rex*, the *General Prologue of the Canterbury Tales*, and *Don Quixote*. I was surprised when my drama instructor mentioned that the Ancient Greeks not only invented the play but elevated it to a level no playwright has ever since attained. I was impressed when my Chaucer professor announced that *Canterbury Tales* is the first poem by a named author in our language and, even today, remains our most complex and brilliant one. I was astonished when my fiction lecturer stated that *Don Quixote* is both the first modern novel and the greatest ever written.

Do we detect a trend here? In exact opposition to the values of our current age, the study of literature reveals that the earliest is often still the best and most highly prized. Perhaps the reason might lie in the definition of literature's sphere. Whereas most academic subjects are rather exact studies (biology as the study of living organisms; engineering as the study of managing engines) literature has, to my mind, a less specific but more glorious study: literature is the study of what it is to be a human being. With this as its special province of knowledge it's no wonder that the earlier writers stand supreme.

Their themes – sacrifice, revenge, idealism, passion, father-son conflict, betrayal, religious doubt – had been experienced by mankind for thousands of years before even the earliest writers approached the subjects artistically. The very complexity of the modern era hinders our writers from concentrating on men and women's most universal and, therefore, most moving struggles. The ancient world had a greater, simpler context, and its writers seemed to know everything worth knowing.

Today, with the help of computers, we can specialize *ad infinitum* so that writers and readers can learn more and more about less and less until we may end up with the dubious distinction of knowing absolutely everything about nothing.

But Sophocles, Chaucer, and Cervantes, our literary Rich Uncles (with the first and best of everything) bequeath to us the eternal verities of human nature which connect us to our most ancient ancestors and secure us irrevocably to our most distant descendants.

Of all God's creatures, there is only one that cannot be made slave of the lash. That one is the cat. If man could be crossed with the cat it would improve the man, but it would deteriorate the cat. --- Mark Twain

Dick Whittington and His Cat

By Joseph Jacobs

In the reign of the famous King Edward III, there was a little boy called Dick Whittington, whose father and mother died when he was very young. As poor Dick was not old enough to work, he was very badly off; he got but little for his dinner, and sometimes nothing at all for his breakfast; for the people who lived in the village were very poor indeed, and could not spare him much more than the parings of potatoes, and now and then a hard crust of bread.

Now Dick had heard a great many very strange things about the great city called London; for the country people at that time thought that folks in London were all fine gentlemen and ladies; and that there was singing and music there all day long; and that the streets were all paved with gold.

One day a large waggon and eight horses, all with bells at their heads, drove through the village while Dick was standing by the signpost. He thought that this waggon must be going to the fine town of London; so he took courage, and asked the waggoner to let him walk with him by the side of the waggon. As soon as the waggoner heard that poor Dick had no father or mother, and saw by his ragged clothes that he could not be worse off than he was, he told him he might go if he would, so off they set together.

So Dick got safe to London, and was in such a hurry to see the fine streets paved all over with gold, that he did not even stay to thank the kind waggoner; but ran off as fast as his legs would carry him, through many of the streets, thinking every moment to come to those that were paved with gold; for Dick had seen a guinea three times in his own little village, and remembered what a deal of money it brought in change; so he thought he had nothing to do but to take up some little bits of the pavement, and should then have as much money as he could wish for.

Poor Dick ran till he was tired, and had quite forgot his friend the waggoner; but at last, finding it grow dark, and that every way he turned he saw nothing but dirt instead of gold, he, sat down in a dark corner and cried himself to sleep.

Little Dick was all night in the streets; and next morning, being very hungry, he got up and walked about, and asked everybody he met to give him a halfpenny to keep him from starving; but nobody stayed to answer him, and only two or three gave him a halfpenny; so that the poor boy was soon quite weak and faint for the want of victuals.

In this distress he asked charity of several people, and one of them said crossly: "Go to work, for an idle rogue." "That I will," says Dick, "I will to go work for you, if you will let me." But the man only cursed at him and went on.

At last a good-natured looking gentleman saw how hungry he looked. "Why don't you go to work, my lad?" said he to Dick. "That I would, but I do not know how to get any," answered Dick. "If you are willing, come along with me," said the gentleman, and took him to a hayfield, where Dick worked briskly, and lived merrily till the hay was made.

After this he found himself as badly off as before; and being almost starved again, he laid himself down at the door of Mr. Fitzwarren, a rich merchant. Here he was soon seen by the cook-maid, who was an ill- tempered creature, and happened just then to be very busy dressing dinner for her master and mistress; so she called out to poor Dick: "What business have you there, you lazy rogue? There is nothing else but beggars; if you do not take yourself away, we will see how you will like a sousing of some dishwater; I have some here hot enough to make you jump."

Just at that time Mr. Fitzwarren himself came home to dinner; and when he saw a dirty ragged boy lying at the door, he said to him: "Why do you lie there, my boy? You seem old enough to work; I am afraid you are inclined to be lazy."

"No, indeed, sir," said Dick to him, "that is not the case, for I would work with all my heart, but I do not know anybody, and I believe I am very sick for the want of food."

"Poor fellow, get up; let me see what ails you." Dick now tried to rise, but was obliged to lie down again, being too weak to stand, for he had not eaten any food for three days, and was no longer able to run about and beg a halfpenny of people in the street. So the kind merchant ordered him to be taken into the house, and have a good dinner given him, and be kept to do what work he was able to do for the cook.

Little Dick would have lived very happy in this good family if it had not been for the ill-natured cook. She used to say: "You are under me, so look sharp; clean the spit and the dripping-pan, make the fires, wind up the jack, and do all the scullery work nimbly, or"—and she would shake the ladle at him. Besides, she was so fond of basting, that when she had no meat to baste, she would baste poor Dick's head and shoulders with a broom, or anything else that happened to fall in her way. At last her ill-usage of him was told to Alice, Mr. Fitzwarren's daughter, who told the cook she should be turned away if she did not treat him kinder.

The behaviour of the cook was now a little better; but besides this Dick had another hardship to get over. His bed stood in a garret, where there were so many holes in the floor and the walls that every night he was tormented with rats and mice. A gentleman having given Dick a penny for cleaning his shoes, he thought he would buy a cat with it. The next day he saw a girl with a cat, and asked her, "Will you let me have that cat for a penny?" The girl said: "Yes, that I will, master, though she is an excellent mouser."

Dick hid his cat in the garret, and always took care to carry a part of his dinner to her; and in a short time he had no more trouble with the rats and mice, but slept quite sound every night.

Soon after this, his master had a ship ready to sail; and as it was the custom that all his servants should have some chance for good fortune as well as himself, he called them all into the parlour and asked them what they would send out.

They all had something that they were willing to venture except poor Dick, who had neither money nor goods, and therefore could send nothing. For this reason he did not come into the parlour with the rest; but Miss Alice guessed what was the matter, and ordered him to be called in. She then said: "I will lay down some money for him, from my own purse;" but her father told her: "This will not do, for it must be something of his own."

When poor Dick heard this, he said: "I have nothing but a cat which I bought for a penny some time since of a little girl."

"Fetch your cat then, my lad," said Mr. Fitzwarren, "and let her go."

Dick went upstairs and brought down poor puss, with tears in his eyes, and gave her to the captain; "For," he said, "I shall now be kept awake all night by the rats and mice." All the company laughed at Dick's odd venture; and Miss Alice, who felt pity for him, gave him some money to buy another cat.

This, and many other marks of kindness shown him by Miss Alice, made the ill-tempered cook jealous of poor Dick, and she began to use him more cruelly than ever, and always made game of him for sending his cat to sea.

She asked him: "Do you think your cat will sell for as much money as would buy a stick to beat you?"

At last poor Dick could not bear this usage any longer, and he thought he would run away from his place; so he packed up his few things, and started very early in the morning, on All-hallows Day, the first of November. He walked as far as Holloway; and there sat down on a stone, which to this day is called "Whittington's Stone," and began to think to himself which road he should take.

While he was thinking what he should do, the Bells of Bow Church, which at that time were only six, began to ring, and their sound seemed to say to him:

"Turn again, Whittington, Thrice Lord Mayor of London."

"Lord Mayor of London!" said he to himself. "Why, to be sure, I would put up with almost anything now, to be Lord Mayor of London, and ride in a fine coach, when I grow to be a man! Well, I will go back, and think nothing of the cuffing and scolding of the old cook, if I am to be Lord Mayor of London at last."

Dick went back, and was lucky enough to get into the house, and set about his work, before the old cook came downstairs.

We must now follow Miss Puss to the coast of Africa. The ship with the cat on board, was a long time at sea; and was at last driven by the winds on a part of the coast of Barbary, where the only people were the Moors, unknown to the English. The people came in great numbers to see the sailors, because they were of different colour to themselves, and treated them civilly; and, when they became better acquainted, were very eager to buy the fine things that the ship was loaded with.

When the captain saw this, he sent patterns of the best things he had to the king of the country; who was so much pleased with them, that he sent for the captain to the palace. Here they were placed, as it is the custom of the country, on rich carpets flowered with gold and silver. The king and queen were seated at the upper end of the room; and a number of dishes were brought in for dinner. They had not sat long, when a vast number of rats and mice rushed in, and devoured all the meat in an instant. The captain wondered at this, and asked if these vermin were not unpleasant.

"Oh yes," said they, "very offensive, and the king would give half his treasure to be freed of them, for they not only destroy his dinner, as you see, but they assault him in his chamber, and even in bed, and so that he is obliged to be watched while he is sleeping, for fear of them."

The captain jumped for joy; he remembered poor Whittington and his cat, and told the king he had a creature on board the ship that would dispatch all these vermin immediately. The king jumped so high at the joy which the news gave him, that his turban dropped off his head. "Bring this creature to me," says he; "vermin are dreadful in a court, and if she will perform what you say, I will load your ship with gold and jewels in exchange for her."

The captain, who knew his business, took this opportunity to set forth the merits of Miss Puss. He told his majesty; "It is not very convenient to part with her, as, when she is gone, the rats and mice may destroy the goods in the ship – but to oblige your majesty, I will fetch her."

"Run, run!" said the queen; "I am impatient to see the dear creature."

Away went the captain to the ship, while another dinner was got ready. He put Puss under his arm, and arrived at the place just in time to see the table full of rats. When the cat saw them, she did not wait for bidding, but jumped out of the captain's arms, and in a few minutes laid almost all the rats and mice dead at her feet. The rest of them in their fright scampered away to their holes.

The king was quite charmed to get rid so easily of such plagues, and the queen desired that the creature who had done them so great a kindness might be brought to her, that she might look at her. Upon which the captain called: "Pussy, pussy, pussy!" and she came to him. He then presented her to the queen, who started back, and was afraid to touch a creature who had made such a havoc among the rats and mice. However, when the captain stroked the cat and called: "Pussy, pussy," the queen also touched her and cried: "Putty, putty," for she had not learned English. He then put her down on the queen's lap, where she purred and played with her majesty's hand, and then purred herself to sleep.

The king, having seen the exploits of Mrs. Puss, and being informed that her kittens would stock the whole country, and keep it free from rats, bargained with the captain for the whole ship's cargo, and then gave him ten times as much for the cat as all the rest amounted to.

The captain then took leave of the royal party, and set sail with a fair wind for England, and after a happy voyage arrived safe in London.

One morning, early, Mr. Fitzwarren had just come to his counting-house and seated himself at the desk, to count over the cash, and settle the business for the day, when somebody came tap, tap, at the door. "Who's there?" said Mr. Fitzwarren. "A friend," answered the other; "I come to bring you good news of your ship—*Unicorn*." The merchant, bustling up in such a hurry that he forgot his gout, opened the door, and who should he see waiting but the captain and factor, with a cabinet of jewels, and a bill of lading; when he looked at this the merchant lifted up his eyes and thanked Heaven for sending him such a prosperous voyage.

They then told the story of the cat, and showed the rich present that the king and queen had sent for her to poor Dick. As soon as the merchant heard this, he called out to his servants:

"Go send him in, and tell him of his fame;
Pray call him Mr. Whittington by name."

Mr. Fitzwarren now showed himself to be a good man; for when some of his servants said so great a treasure was too much for him, he answered: "God forbid I should deprive him of the value of a single penny, it is his own, and he shall have it to a farthing." He then sent for Dick, who at that time was scouring pots for the cook, and was quite dirty. He would have excused himself from coming into the counting-house, saying, "The room is swept, and my shoes are dirty and full of hob-nails." But the merchant ordered him to come in.

Mr. Fitzwarren ordered a chair to be set for him, and so he began to think they were making game of him, at the same time said to them: "Do not play tricks with a poor simple boy, but let me go down again, if you please, to my work."

"Indeed, Mr. Whittington," said the merchant, "we are all quite in earnest with you, and I most heartily rejoice in the news that these gentlemen have brought you; for the captain has sold your cat to the King of Barbary, and brought you in return for her more riches than I possess in the whole world; and I wish you may long enjoy them!"

Mr. Fitzwarren then told the men to open the great treasure they had brought with them; and said: "Mr. Whittington has nothing to do but to put it in some place of safety."

Poor Dick hardly knew how to behave himself for joy. He begged his master to take what part of it he pleased, since he owed it all to his kindness. "No, no," answered Mr. Fitzwarren, "this is all your own; and I have no doubt but you will use it well."

Dick next asked his mistress, and then Miss Alice, to accept a part of his good fortune; but they would not, and at the same time told him they felt great joy at his good success. But this poor fellow was too kind-hearted to keep it all to himself; so he made a present to the captain, the mate, and the rest of Mr. Fitzwarren's servants; and even to the ill-natured old cook.

After this Mr. Fitzwarren advised him to send for a proper tailor and get himself dressed like a gentleman; and told him he was welcome to live in his house till he could provide himself with a better.

When Whittington's face was washed, his hair curled, his hat cocked, and he was dressed in a nice suit of clothes he was as handsome and genteel as any young man who visited at Mr.

Fitzwarren's; so that Miss Alice, who had once been so kind to him, and thought of him with pity, now looked upon him as fit to be her sweetheart; and the more so, no doubt, because Whittington was now always thinking what he could do to oblige her, and making her the prettiest presents that could be.

Mr. Fitzwarren soon saw their love for each other, and proposed to join them in marriage; and to this they both readily agreed. A day for the wedding was soon fixed; and they were attended to church by the Lord Mayor, the court of aldermen, the sheriffs, and a great number of the richest merchants in London, whom they afterwards treated with a very rich feast.

History tells us that Mr. Whittington and his lady lived in great splendour, and were very happy. They had several children. He was Sheriff of London, thrice Lord Mayor, and received the honour of knighthood by Henry V.

He entertained this king and his queen at dinner after his conquest of France so grandly, that the king said "Never had prince such a subject;" when Sir Richard heard this, he said: "Never had subject such a prince."

The figure of Sir Richard Whittington with his cat in his arms, carved in stone, was to be seen till the year 1780 over the archway of the old prison of Newgate, which he built for criminals.

You'll notice that both of these very short works in this chapter present a rather SOUR view of the world. My essay attempts to take a most sour personal experience — lost luggage at the airport — and turn it into the foundation of pure comedy. I hope you feel that I succeeded.

Flying so frequently to my lecture sites, I'm always landing at airports where I know nobody in the town. Be it Fargo or Fresno, as I exit the plane, I realize that the eager faces at the gate awaiting loved ones will look right past me to scan for that one special person. If I deplane early the faces that meet mine are happy and full of anticipation; if I'm one of the last, the faces look rather grim and anxious, fearing that their loved ones never made the flight.

Ironically, this very ritual is repeated by me a few minutes later at the level below in that high suspense area known as Baggage Claim. But now *I'm* the eager face in front of the conveyor belt anxiously scanning each piece of luggage as it moves into sight. Like those at the gate awaiting loved ones, I am at first all optimistic anticipation, hoping my familiar blue Hartmann suit bag will pop into view immediately, thus insuring a quick exit to my rental car. But when I've waited fifteen minutes and still not glimpsed my piece of luggage, my expression takes on the same fear and trepidation for my bag that those people at the gate had for their missing loved ones.

I've experienced lost luggage, late luggage and lacerated luggage, but my most ghastly experience was in Dallas years ago. Waiting at the luggage carousel, I remember my initial disgusted reaction when the first bag to appear on the belt was none other than a large brown garbage bag, complete with loose yellow tie-string and bulging sides. "Has it come to this?" I remember thinking, "that the quality of air passengers has sunk so low that some prefer Hefty to Louis Vuitton?" As the final degradation, I noticed as the bag passed by, two pairs of underwear could be seen protruding through a large rip in the plastic. I admit that from that moment I used one eye to spot my own bag and the other to see who in the world would claim the garbage bag.

By coincidence, nobody claimed the Hefty nor did my bag ever come into sight. Finally, I was the only one left at the carousel and the Hefty was the only thing circling. Not until then did I notice something appallingly familiar about the Fruit-of-the-Loom jockeys and something depressingly blue and Hartmannesque deep within the now slowly opening trash bag.

A revelation flashed upon me: somehow my bag must have been destroyed and the handlers had tossed it and my orphaned belongings in their garbage bag of choice for me to claim. I was both furious and, idiotically, humiliated that my anonymous underpants had been on display for all of Flight #722 to snicker at in public.

Yes, the airline replaced the bag. I asked the agent how this could have happened, but she only shrugged and rolled her eyes. Visions of gorillas and Samsonites wrestling together danced through my mind.

I noticed that my exposed underwear had what looked like airplane grease on them. Rather than washing my dirty laundry in public, so to speak, I simply abandoned them in an airport trash container. As I wearily wandered to my rental car, I found myself humming a familiar tune. It was the Tony Bennett classic. He had left his heart in San Francisco; I had left my dirty drawers in Dallas.

King o' the Cats

By Joseph Jacobs

One winter's evening the sexton's wife was sitting by the fireside with her big black cat, Old Tom, on the other side, both half asleep and waiting for the master to come home. They waited and they waited, but still he didn't come, till at last he came rushing in, calling out, "Who's Tommy Tildrum?" in such a wild way that both his wife and his cat stared at him to know what was the matter.

"Why, what's the matter?" said his wife, "and why do you want to know who Tommy Tildrum is?"

"Oh, I've had such an adventure. I was digging away at old Mr. Fordyce's grave when I suppose I must have dropped asleep, and only woke up by hearing a cat's "Miaou."

"Miaou!" said Old Tom in answer.

"Yes, just like that! So I looked over the edge of the grave, and what do you think I saw?"

"Now, how can I tell?" said the sexton's wife.

"Why, nine black cats all like our friend Tom here, all with a white spot on their chestesses. And what do you think they were carrying? Why, a small coffin covered with a black velvet pall, and on the pall was a small coronet all of gold, and at every third step they took they cried all together, "Miaou."

"Miaou!" said Old Tom again.

"Yes, just like that!" said the Sexton; "and as they came nearer and nearer to me I could see them more distinctly, because their eyes shone out with a sort of green light. Well, they all came towards me, eight of them carrying the coffin, and the biggest cat of all walking in front for all the world like—but look at our Tom, how he's looking at me. You'd think he knew all I was saying."

"Go on, go on," said his wife; "never mind Old Tom."

"Well, as I was a-saying, they came towards me slowly and solemnly, and at every third step crying all together, "Miaou!"

"Miaou!" said Old Tom again.

"Yes, just like that, till they came and stood right opposite Mr. Fordyce's grave, where I was, when they all stood still and looked straight at me. I did feel queer, that I did! But look at Old Tom; he's looking at me just like they did."

"Go on, go on," said his wife; "never mind Old Tom."

"Where was I? Oh, they all stood still looking at me, when the one that wasn't carrying the coffin came forward and, staring straight at me, said to me -- yes, I tell 'ee, -- said to me, with a squeaky voice, 'Tell Tom Tildrum that Tim Toldrum's dead,' and that's why I asked you if you knew who Tom Tildrum was, for how can I tell Tom Tildrum Tim Toldrum's dead if I don't know who Tom Tildrum is?"

"Look at Old Tom, look at Old Tom!" screamed his wife.

And well he might look, for Tom was swelling and Tom was staring, and at last Tom shrieked out, "What—old Tim dead! Then I'm the King o' the Cats!" and rushed up the chimney and was never more seen.

Thousands of years ago, cats were worshipped as gods. Cats have never forgotten this. --- Anonymous

The Cat And The Youth

By Ambrose Bierce

A Cat fell in love with a handsome Young Man, and entreated Venus to change her into a woman.

"I should think," said Venus, "you might make so trifling a change without bothering me. However, be a woman."

Afterward, wishing to see if the change were complete, Venus caused a mouse to approach, whereupon the woman shrieked and made such a show of herself that the Young Man would not marry her.

> *Since this chapter is devoted exclusively to poetry, I chose an essay that climaxes with the most delightful Medieval poem in our language.*

My parents probably knew from my earliest age that I was going to be a professor when I grew up. Their clue would not have come from any particular academic brilliance nor from an unusual love of learning but rather from the one quality I possessed that the general public has always associated with professors: absent-mindedness.

As a child, I never met a mitten, jacket, nor gym shoe that I liked enough to remember to take with me when I boarded the school bus at the end of the day. If it could be left behind, it was; if it could be misplaced, I misplaced it; if it wasn't attached, it was in the Lost and Found (or, all too often, the Lost and Never Found). I remember being genuinely surprised when I learned in junior high school that my head was attached to my body by muscles and spinal cord rather than by a metal coil. After all, I had been told by my entire family since I was five: "Elliot, if your head weren't screwed on to your shoulders, you'd forget it, too."

My absent-mindedness has continued into middle age and so I consider it ironic that my profession as a national lecturer today depends as much on a good memory as on any other talent. When I prepared and memorized my first Dickens lecture in 1974, I worried that I couldn't recite it for fifty minutes without forgetting a crucial phrase or two. Now it is thirty years later, and I am lecturing on seventy different topics – at least half of which are memorized and all approximately fifty minutes long. Thus, I've committed to memory approximately 1800 minutes or thirty solid hours of lectures.

I admit to having occasional nightmares when I dream of confusing my Mark Twain talk with my Emily Dickinson lecture and end up telling an audience of scholars, that Samuel Clemens grew up in Hannibal, Missouri, but lived most of his life as a reclusive spinster in a white dress in Amherst, Massachusetts. But so far I have yet to forget a chunk of my speech nor have I married off a Brontë sister to Edgar Allan Poe.

Up to this point, never the Twain did meet Ms. Emily nor any other inappropriate lecture lady.

Most of my talks also contain memorizations within the speech itself since I'm usually quoting from some poem or other literary work of a particular author – "*The Raven*" for Poe or Kipling's "*If*" for my conclusion of Winston Churchill. Even as a child I felt a special thrill when I had memorized a poem. The expression "to know by heart" is an apt one, for when we merely read a poem we engage our mind, but when we memorize it, we do seem to make it our own by directly taking it into our hearts.

And speaking of memory, I shall never forget a lecture I gave years ago to a group of seniors in high school in a rural county of North Carolina. The teacher had requested that I speak on Geoffrey Chaucer. Of course, I could not help but recite the famous opening fourteen lines of *The Canterbury Tales* in the original Middle English. As I began, I heard a rather loud mumbling among the students. Imagine my shock – and glee – when I realized that they were reciting the lines with me in accents they had learned from their teacher. There we were – a middle-aged English professor and over one hundred eighteen-year-olds paying homage to an English author who, more than 600 years ago (about 1392) penned a description of the month of April so moving that it has become immortal and, like the spring season it describes, has inspired each new generation with both joy and gratitude for its refreshing beauty.

There was a rare communion in that North Carolina high school auditorium that day. I know that no matter how absent-minded I may become in later years, that particular memory will never be absent from this mind. Like Chaucer's poem, it remains ever fresh to inspire me with the renewal that comes with spring – and with teaching.

The General Prologue from *The Canterbury Tales*

(Middle English)

Whan that aprill with his shoures soote
The droghte of march hath perced to the roote,
And bathed every veyne in swich licour
Of which vertu engendred is the flour;
Whan zephirus eek with his sweete breeth
Inspired hath in every holt and heeth
Tendre croppes, and the yonge sonne
Hath in the ram his halve cours yronne,
And smale foweles maken melodye,
That slepen al the nyght with open ye
(so priketh hem nature in hir corages);
Thanne longen folk to goon on pilgrimages.

(Modern English)

When April with his showers sweet with fruit
The drought of March has pierced unto the root
And bathed each vein with liquor that has power
To generate therein and sire the flower;
When Zephyr also has, with his sweet breath,
Quickened again, in every holt and heath,
The tender shoots and buds, and the young sun
Into the Ram one half his course has run,
And many little birds make melody
That sleep through all the night with open eye
(So Nature pricks them on to ramp and rage)-
Then do folk long to go on pilgrimage.

The Owl and the Pussycat

By Edward Lear

I.

The Owl and the Pussy-cat went to sea
    In a beautiful pea green boat,
They took some honey, and plenty of money,
    Wrapped up in a five pound note.
The Owl looked up to the stars above,
    And sang to a small guitar,
'O lovely Pussy! O Pussy my love,
    What a beautiful Pussy you are,
        You are,
        You are!
What a beautiful Pussy you are!'

II.

Pussy said to the Owl, 'You elegant fowl!
    How charmingly sweet you sing!
O let us be married! too long we have tarried:
    But what shall we do for a ring?'
They sailed away, for a year and a day,
    To the land where the Bong-tree grows
And there in a wood a Piggy-wig stood
    With a ring at the end of his nose,
        His nose,
        His nose,
With a ring at the end of his nose.

III.

'Dear pig, are you willing to sell for one shilling
    Your ring?' Said the Piggy, 'I will.'
So they took it away, and were married next day
    By the Turkey who lives on the hill.

They dined on mince, and slices of quince,
    Which they ate with a runcible spoon;
And hand in hand, on the edge of the sand,
    They danced by the light of the moon,
        The moon,
        The moon,
They danced by the light of the moon.

Lear's Unfinished Posthumous Follow-Up...

The Children of the Owl and the Pussycat

By Edward Lear

Our mother was the Pussycat, our father was the Owl,
And so we're partly little beasts and partly little fowl,
The brothers of our family have feathers and they hoot,
While all the sisters dress in fur and have long tails to boot.
    We all believe that little mice,
    For food are singularly nice.
Our mother died long years ago. She was a lovely cat.
Her tail was 5 feet long, and grey with stripes, but what of that?
In Sila forest on the East of fair Calabria's shore
She tumbled from a lofty tree—none ever saw her more.
Our owly father long was ill from sorrow and surprise,
But with the feathers of his tail he wiped his weeping eyes.
And in the hollow of a tree in Sila's inmost maze
We made a happy home and there we pass our obvious days.

From Reggian Cosenza many owls about us flit
And bring us worldly news for which we do not care a bit.
We watch the sun each morning rise, beyond Tarento's strait;
We go out _____ before it gets too late;

And when the evening shades begin to lengthen from the trees
_____ as sure as bees is bees.

We wander up and down the shore _____

Or tumble over head and heels, but never, never more
Can see the far Gromboolian plains _____

Or weep as we could once have wept o'er many a vanished scene:

This is the way our father moans—he is so very green.

Our father still preserves his voice, and when he sees a star
He often sings _____to that original guitar.

_____

_____

The pot in which our parents took the honey in their boat,
But all the money has been spent, beside the £5 note.
The owls who come and bring us news are often _____
Because we take no interest in poltix of the day.)

The _____ are parts Lear didn't finish.

Why don't you complete it for him?

Meow is like aloha – it can mean anything. --- Hank Ketchum

The Cat And The Moon

By W.B. Yeats

The cat went here and there
And the moon spun round like a top
And the nearest kin of the moon,
The creeping cat, looked up.

Black Minnaloushe stared at the moon,
For, wander and wail as he would,
The pure cold light in the sky
Troubled his animal blood.
Minnaloushe runs in the grass
Lifting his delicate feet.

Do you dance, Minnaloushe, do you dance?
When two close kindred meet,
What better than call a dance?
Maybe the moon may learn,
Tired of that courtly fashion
A new dance turn.

Minnaloushe creeps through the grass
From moonlit place to place,
The sacred moon overhead
Has taken a new phase.

Does Minnaloushe know that his pupils
Will pass from change to change,
And that from round to crescent,
From crescent to round they range?

Minnaloushe creeps through the grass
Alone, important and wise,
And lifts to the changing moon
His changing eyes.

On a Cat, Ageing

By Alexander Gray

He blinks upon the hearth rug,
And yawns in deep content,
Accepting all the comforts
That Providence has sent.

Loud he purrs and louder,
In one glad hymn of praise
For all the night's adventures,
For quiet restful days.

Life will go on forever,
With all that cat can wish,
Warmth and the glad procession
Of fish and milk and fish.

Only - the thought disturbs him -
He's noticed once or twice
The times are somehow breeding
A nimbler breed of mice.

She Sights a Bird – She Chuckles (Poem #507)

By Emily Dickinson

She sights a Bird—she chuckles—
She flattens—then she crawls—
She runs without the look of feet—
Her eyes increase to Balls—

Her jaws stir—twitching—hungry—
Her Teeth can hardly stand—
She leaps, but Robin leaped the first—
Ah, Pussy, of the Sand,

The Hopes so juicy ripening—
You almost bathed your Tongue—
When Bliss disclosed a hundred Toes—
And fled with every one—

> *Although the author Charles Perrault was French, he collected fairy tales from all cultures. This one, as the character Master of Carabus would imply, is a Spanish tale. My essay deals with the American author Ernest Hemingway, but my emphasis on bullfighting is as Spanish as the Master of Carabus.*

This last year of the twentieth century marks a significant literary commemoration. It was one hundred years ago – on July 21, 1899 – that Ernest Hemingway was born in Oak Park, Illinois. As our century ends, Hemingway's stature continues to rise. He now stands virtually alone as the single-most important personality in modern American fiction. Granted, William Faulkner, F. Scott Fitzgerald, and John Steinbeck all rival him as novelists but certainly not as personalities. Like Lord Byron before him, Hemingway was as equally famous for *who* he was as for what he wrote. The Hemingway hero in fiction – brave, stoic, aloof, and sensitive – possessed the very traits that Hemingway himself tried to project as his public persona.

How well he succeeded in this attempt is still in question. Even though I was only thirteen years old, I vividly remember that Sunday morning of June 30, 1961, when it was announced that Ernest Hemingway had committed suicide at his home in Ketchum, Idaho. His failing health (a depressing combination of diabetes, insomnia, hypertension, kidney trouble, and glaucoma) was cited as a possible reason for taking his life. Here was a man who defined the term "courage" so succinctly and brilliantly as "grace under pressure," but when the pressures of advancing age undermined him physically he failed to possess the courage to struggle on.

The Hemingway personality was even an influence on my childhood. Hemingway's passion for bullfighting introduced so many Americans to the joy of the Spanish sport that it even filtered down to the suburbs of Indianapolis when I was a child in the 1950s. My best friend Andy and I spent hours in our backyards engaging in bullfights of our own imagining. They were a unique mixture of sport and farce. With my – shall we say – **directive** personality, I carefully chose my childhood friends based on their passivity and gullibility. Thus, I always starred as the gallant matador with Andy playing the supporting role of *El Toro*. I used a yardstick for my sword which, ironically, turned out to be a most literary weapon. It was emblazoned with the name of the largest hardware store in Indianapolis which happened to be Vonnegut's, owned by the parents of Kurt himself, our great hometown author. Andy would raise his arms over his lowered head and wiggle his index and middle finger to signify the bull's twitching horns. What he lacked in Taurean stature, he more than made up for with his astonishingly adenoidal snorts.

He would charge at me when I boldly waved the red cape in front of him. Toreador capes being in short supply at my house, we were reduced to pilfering my sister's fiery red skirt from her closet. Alas, it had a large dancing poodle on it (as many 50's skirts did) which detracted somewhat from the gravity of the blood sport. As often as not, Andy would butt into the skirt before I could whip it aside; therefore, when we clandestinely returned it to my sister's closet it was in desperate need of dry-cleaning from the stains of pomade (we called it "butch-wax") which Andy had applied liberally to his crew cut to keep it vertical.

I mention all this because my heart was never into the macho bullfighting drama, probably due to my utter lack of athletic grace. As a child, I would have had to have been twice as good in sports as I was to be considered merely uncoordinated. When the Hemingway-inspired fad for bullfighting swept through my elementary school, I would never have confessed to the name of my favorite literary steer.

But I do now. It was Ferdinand, the bull from the famous Spanish fairy tale who would rather smell the marigolds than slash the matadors. My favorite part was when his mother suggested that he run and play sporting games with the other little bulls:

"But Ferdinand would shake his head. 'I like it better where I can sit quietly and smell the flowers.' His mother saw that he was not lonesome, and because she was an understanding mother, even though she was a cow, she let him just sit there and be happy."

I have a mother like that. After fruitless attempts to sign me up for Little League, my mother let me cultivate my own solitary garden. But my flowers had pages rather than petals.

They were the hundreds of books I inhaled (perhaps "ingested" is the better image) as a child. And eventually they led me to a love of Hemingway, Jack London, and other virile authors whose athletic prowess I could not emulate but whose love of the sporting world I could appreciate due to the magic of their enthralling stories. And I've been bullish on books ever since.

There are two means of refuge from the miseries of life: music and cats. --- Albert Schweitzer

The Master Cat; or, Puss in Boots

By Charles Perrault

There was a miller whose only inheritance to his three sons was his mill, his donkey, and his cat. The division was soon made. They hired neither a clerk nor an attorney, for they would have eaten up all the poor patrimony. The eldest took the mill, the second the donkey, and the youngest nothing but the cat.

The poor young fellow was quite comfortless for having received so little. "My brothers," said he, "may make a handsome living by joining their shares together; but, for my part, after I have eaten up my cat, and made myself a muff from his skin, I must then die of hunger."

The cat, who heard all this, but pretended otherwise, said to him with a grave and serious air, "Do not be so concerned, my good master. If you will but give me a bag, and have a pair of boots made for me, that I may scamper through the dirt and the brambles, then you shall see that you are not so poorly off with me as you imagine."

The cat's master did not build very much upon what he said. However, he had often seen him play a great many cunning tricks to catch rats and mice, such as hanging by his heels, or hiding himself in the meal, and pretending to be dead; so he did take some hope that he might give him some help in his miserable condition.

After receiving what he had asked for, the cat gallantly pulled on the boots and slung the bag about his neck. Holding its drawstrings in his forepaws, he went to a place where there was a great abundance of rabbits. He put some bran and greens into his bag, then stretched himself out as if he were dead. He thus waited for some young rabbits, not yet acquainted with the deceits of the world, to come and look into his bag.

He had scarcely lain down before he had what he wanted. A rash and foolish young rabbit jumped into his bag, and the master cat, immediately closed the strings, then took and killed him without pity.

Proud of his prey, he went with it to the palace, and asked to speak with his majesty. He was shown upstairs into the king's apartment, and, making a low bow, said to him, "Sir, I have brought you a rabbit from my noble lord, the Marquis of Carabas" (for that was the title which the cat was pleased to give his master).

"Tell your master," said the king, "that I thank him, and that I am very pleased with his gift."

Another time he went and hid himself in a grain field. He again held his bag open, and when a brace of partridges ran into it, he drew the strings, and caught them both. He presented these to the king, as he had done before with the rabbit. The king, in like manner, received the partridges with great pleasure, and gave him a tip. The cat continued, from time to time for two or three months, to take game to his majesty from his master.

One day, when he knew for certain that the king would be taking a drive along the riverside with his daughter, the most beautiful princess in the world, he said to his master, "If you will follow my advice your fortune is made. All you must do is to go and bathe yourself in the river at the place I show you, then leave the rest to me."

The young man did what the cat advised him to, without knowing why. While he was bathing the king passed by, and the cat began to cry out, "Help! Help! My Lord Marquis of Carabas is going to be drowned."

At this noise the king put his head out of the coach window, and, finding it was the cat who had so often brought him such good game, he commanded his guards to run immediately to the assistance of his lordship the Marquis of Carabas. While they were drawing the poor Marquis out of the river, the cat came up to the coach and told the king that, while his master was bathing, some rogues had come by and stolen his clothes, even though he had cried out, "Thieves! Thieves!" several times, as loud as he could. In truth, the cunning cat had hidden the clothes under a large stone.

The king immediately commanded the officers of his wardrobe to run and fetch one of his best suits for the Lord Marquis of Carabas.

The king received him very courteously. And, because the king's fine clothes gave him a striking appearance (for he was very handsome and well proportioned), the king's daughter took a secret inclination to him. The Marquis of Carabas had only to cast two or three respectful and somewhat tender glances at her but she fell head over heels in love with him. The king asked him to enter the coach and join them on their drive.

The cat, quite overjoyed to see how his project was succeeding, ran on ahead. Meeting some countrymen who were mowing a meadow, he said to them, "My good fellows, if you do not tell the king that the meadow you are mowing belongs to my Lord Marquis of Carabas, you shall be chopped up like mincemeat."

The king did not fail to ask the mowers whose meadow it was that they were mowing.

"It belongs to my Lord Marquis of Carabas," they answered altogether, for the cat's threats had frightened them.

"You see, sir," said the Marquis, "this is a meadow which never fails to yield a plentiful harvest every year."

The master cat, still running on ahead, met with some reapers, and said to them, "My good fellows, if you do not tell the king that all this grain belongs to the Marquis of Carabas, you shall be chopped up like mincemeat."

The king, who passed by a moment later, asked them whose grain it was that they were reaping.

"It belongs to my Lord Marquis of Carabas," replied the reapers, which pleased both the king and the marquis. The king congratulated him for his fine harvest. The master cat continued to run ahead and said the same words to all he met. The king was astonished at the vast estates of the Lord Marquis of Carabas.

The master cat came at last to a stately castle, the lord of which was an ogre, the richest that had ever been known. All the lands which the king had just passed by belonged to this castle. The cat, who had taken care to inform himself who this ogre was and what he could do, asked to speak with him, saying he could not pass so near his castle without having the honor of paying his respects to him.

The ogre received him as civilly as an ogre could do, and invited him to sit down. "I have heard," said the cat, "that you are able to change yourself into any kind of creature that you have a mind to. You can, for example, transform yourself into a lion, an elephant, or the like."

"That is true," answered the ogre very briskly; "and to convince you, I shall now become a lion."

The cat was so terrified at the sight of a lion so near him that he leaped onto the roof, which caused him even more difficulty, because his boots were of no use at all to him in walking on the tiles. However, the ogre resumed his natural form, and the cat came down, saying that he had been very frightened indeed.

"I have further been told," said the cat, "that you can also transform yourself into the smallest of animals, for example, a rat or a mouse. But I can scarcely believe that. I must admit to you that I think that that would be quite impossible."

"Impossible!" cried the ogre. "You shall see!"

He immediately changed himself into a mouse and began to run about the floor. As soon as the cat saw this, he fell upon him and ate him up.

Meanwhile the king, who saw this fine castle of the ogre's as he passed, decided to go inside. The cat, who heard the noise of his majesty's coach running over the drawbridge, ran out and said to the king, "Your majesty is welcome to this castle of my Lord Marquis of Carabas."

"What! my Lord Marquis," cried the king, "and does this castle also belong to you? There can be nothing finer than this court and all the stately buildings which surround it. Let us go inside, if you don't mind."

The Marquis gave his hand to the princess, and followed the king, who went first. They passed into a spacious hall, where they found a magnificent feast, which the ogre had prepared for his friends, who were coming to visit him that very day, but dared not to enter, knowing the king was there.

His Majesty was perfectly charmed with the good qualities of my Lord Marquis of Carabas, as was his daughter, who had fallen violently in love with him, and, seeing the vast estate he possessed, said to him, after having drunk five or six glasses, "It will be your own fault, my Lord Marquis, if you do not become my son-in-law."

The Marquis, making several low bows, accepted the honor which His Majesty conferred upon him, and forthwith, that very same day, married the princess.

The cat became a great lord, and never again ran after mice, except for entertainment.

> *My essay will argue that the greatest characters in literature all have strong souls or what literary critics call strong Essential Selves. Even though the literature in this chapter is a fairy tale with cats for hero and heroine, they could hardly be better examples of strongly entwined essential selves than if they were Romeo and Juliet.*

The Romans, who named the month of January, certainly recognized it as a time of transition. They named it after Janus, the god who had two faces so that he could look both forward and backward at the same time. This past January has been especially transitional since, for the first time in over a decade, our government changes from one political party to the other. Ever since early November of last year, the media have bombarded us with articles and stories about transition teams and the man who created them and bore the very transitional title of President-Elect.

But even with all of this emphasis, we still tend to forget that as human beings our lives are, above all else, ones of transition. As ironists have pointed out for hundreds of years, the only permanent truth in this strange world of ours is that everything always changes.

The Bible recognizes this mutability in human affairs. Although the King James version frequently states "It came to pass," it does not, to my knowledge, ever state "It came to stay."

This point was vividly brought home to me last month when I was glancing at that page in the newspaper reserved for the Ultimate Transition: the obituaries. My eye was caught by a picture of a very beautiful woman in her mid or late thirties. Even before I started to read the article I felt a vague sadness that a person so young and vibrant had died. Imagine my surprise when the first sentence revealed that the woman had just died at the age of 91!

At first I was somewhat amused at the vanity of the deceased's family for putting a picture in the newspaper which could have easily been mistaken for the woman's granddaughter. But then I realized that since this woman's life was now over and was being reviewed as a whole in the obituary, why would a likeness of her at age 90 be any more appropriate than one taken in her thirties? Is the most recent picture we take somehow more accurate than any other? Since life is always a series of changes, who can determine which photograph – snapped in merely one second of a life (if lived to age 91) that will contain 2,869,778,000—is most representative?

Great literature has not only recognized this peculiar and precarious human condition of change, but it has addressed it in two important ways. First, believe it or not, the structure and theme of every great novel or short story you have ever read depended more upon a character's transition than upon any other element. All great stories begin with a character placed in a situation that demands change; all great stories end immediately after that change has been accomplished.

That's why a title such as *Gone With The Wind* is so satisfying. It captures both the fragile nature of the antebellum South and the obliterating change that the war will bring. Dickens' wonderful title *Great Expectations* summarizes in two words both Pip's dream of a big change for the better and the bitterness he'll experience when that dream proves shallow and false. Change is the prime catalyst for all plots. Each story is a journey from initial innocence to ultimate maturity. Each life is too.

But great literature also teaches us that amid all the chaotic transitions that inundate our lives, there is one element that can be unchanging. And that is our inner-self, that solitary and unseen combination of inherited and learned traits that comprise our unique personality. In religion, it is called the Soul; in literature, it is called the Essential Self. It is the ElliotEngelness of me, and the youness of each of you, my readers.

The most impressive and inspirational characters in literature – and in our lives – are those with very strong essential selves, those who bask in a perpetual summer of always being only themselves. Huck Finn, Jane Eyre, Sidney Carton, and Joe Gargery, the blacksmith, all defy the petty snobbery and fair-weather friendships of proper society and instead stand firm for values and virtues that are timeless. They teach us that even though we must all change in our journey from innocence to experience; certain sterling qualities within us (such as loyalty and empathy) must never change because, if they do, our own character is doomed to diminish to that of a wavering hypocrite. And so it is probably not a coincidence that Janus, the Roman god of change, also happened to be two-faced.

The Cat's Elopement

By Andrew Lang

Once upon a time there lived a cat of marvellous beauty, with a skin as soft and shining as silk, and wise green eyes, that could see even in the dark. His name was Gon, and he belonged to a music teacher, who was so fond and proud of him that he would not have parted with him for anything in the world.

Now not far from the music master's house there dwelt a lady who possessed a most lovely little pussy cat called Koma. She was such a little dear altogether, and blinked her eyes so daintily, and ate her supper so tidily, and when she had finished she licked her pink nose so delicately with her little tongue, that her mistress was never tired of saying, 'Koma, Koma, what should I do without you?'

Well, it happened one day that these two, when out for an evening stroll, met under a cherry tree, and in one moment fell madly in love with each other. Gon had long felt that it was time for him to find a wife, for all the ladies in the neighbourhood paid him so much attention that it made him quite shy; but he was not easy to please, and did not care about any of them. Now, before he had time to think, Cupid had entangled him in his net, and he was filled with love towards Koma. She fully returned his passion, but, like a woman, she saw the difficulties in the way, and consulted sadly with Gon as to the means of overcoming them. Gon entreated his master to set matters right by buying Koma, but her mistress would not part from her. Then the music master was asked to sell Gon to the lady, but he declined to listen to any such suggestion, so everything remained as before.

At length the love of the couple grew to such a pitch that they determined to please themselves, and to seek their fortunes together. So one moonlight night they stole away, and ventured out into an unknown world. All day long they marched bravely on through the sunshine, till they had left their homes far behind them, and towards evening they found themselves in a large park. The wanderers by this time were very hot and tired, and the grass looked very soft and inviting, and the trees cast cool deep shadows, when suddenly an ogre appeared in this Paradise, in the shape of a big, big dog! He came springing towards them showing all his teeth, and Koma shrieked, and rushed up a cherry tree. Gon, however, stood his ground boldly, and prepared to give battle, for he felt that Koma's eyes were upon him, and that he must not run away. But, alas! his courage would have availed him nothing had his enemy once touched him, for he was large and powerful, and very fierce. From her perch in the tree Koma saw it all, and screamed with all her might, hoping that someone would hear, and come to help. Luckily a servant of the princess to whom the park belonged was walking by, and he drove off the dog, and picking up the trembling Gon in his arms, carried him to his mistress.

So poor little Koma was left alone, while Gon was borne away full of trouble, not in the least knowing what to do. Even the attention paid him by the princess, who was delighted with his beauty and pretty ways, did not console him, but there was no use in fighting against fate, and he could only wait and see what would turn up.

The princess, Gon's new mistress, was so good and kind that everybody loved her, and she would have led a happy life, had it not been for a serpent who had fallen in love with her, and was constantly annoying her by his presence. Her servants had orders to drive him away as often as he appeared; but as they were careless, and the serpent very sly, it sometimes happened that he was able to slip past them, and to frighten the princess by appearing before her. One day she was seated in her room, playing on her favourite musical instrument, when she felt something gliding up her sash, and saw her enemy making his way to kiss her cheek. She shrieked and threw herself backwards, and Gon, who had been curled up on a stool at her feet, understood her terror, and with one bound seized the snake by his neck. He gave him one bite and one shake, and flung him on the ground, where he lay, never to worry the princess any more. Then she took Gon in her arms, and praised and caressed him, and saw that he had the nicest bits to eat, and the softest mats to lie on; and he would have had nothing in the world to wish for if only he could have seen Koma again.

Time passed on, and one morning Gon lay before the house door, basking in the sun. He looked lazily at the world stretched out before him, and saw in the distance a big ruffian of a cat teasing and ill-treating quite a little one. He jumped up, full of rage, and chased away the big cat, and then he turned to comfort the little one, when his heart nearly burst with joy to find that it was Koma. At first Koma did not know him again, he had grown so large and stately; but when it dawned upon her who it was, her happiness knew no bounds. And they rubbed their heads and their noses again and again, while their purring might have been heard a mile off.

Paw in paw they appeared before the princess, and told her the story of their life and its sorrows. The princess wept for sympathy, and promised that they should never more be parted, but should live with her to the end of their days. By-and-bye the princess herself got married, and brought a prince to dwell in the palace in the park. And she told him all about her two cats, and how brave Gon had been, and how he had delivered her from her enemy the serpent.

And when the prince heard, he swore they should never leave them, but should go with the princess wherever she went. So it all fell out as the princess wished; and Gon and Koma had many children, and so had the princess, and they all played together, and were friends to the end of their lives.

In a cat's eyes, all things belong to cats. --- English proverb

My essay here, though ultimately upbeat, certainly wanders by the topics of famine and death. Sir Arthur Conan Doyle's story marches directly into impending death and doom to capture our full attention, and its narrator becomes all too well aware of the meaning behind the stark sentence from St. Peter which I quote in the essay: "All flesh is grass."

Charles Dickens, perhaps the most descriptive artist in the history of the novel, did have a deficiency. He was at a loss when it came to describing most plants and flowers. We are told that his favorite flower was the geranium, and it has thus become the cheery symbol for the World Dickens Fellowship today. But probably it was his favorite because it was one of the few he could always recognize. Geraniums blossom throughout his novels; when brides walk down Dickens' aisles, they carry geraniums; when bodies are displayed at his funerals, they're buried with geraniums.

I sympathize with Dickens. I can ask the name of a particular plant or shrub ten times in as many months and yet the next time I see it, the name utterly escapes me. But even with this mental block against many blooms I have always been proud of my intimate relationship with – *grass*.

I'm quite sure why grass has always held a powerful mystique for me. When I was no more than six, my father, who was born and reared in Hungary, told me that at the end of World War I – when he too was six – Hungary suffered such a severe famine that he remembered my grandmother having to prepare an occasional meal with grass, which he vividly recalled eating.

My father eating grass. The thought of it helped make me that rare child with catholic tastes for food and not one finicky aversion, not even for spinach since at least it wasn't quite grass.

But then in fifth grade, my awful feelings about grass turned into pure awe, thanks to a wonderful teacher who liked literature but loved science. This was Miss Walls. First, she taught us that my two very favorite foods – steak and whipped cream (I said my tastes were catholic, not sophisticated) – were both created because cows ate grass and converted it into the most unlikely foods.

But what really impressed me was her lesson on wheat. Who would have guessed that it too is just a humble grass and, as with the cow, it can be converted into the most unlikely and most essential food of all – bread? Within our bread, Miss Walls taught us, is protein which we humans convert to protoplasm, the essence of life. And when we die, she reassuringly continued, that protoplasm reverts back to protein in the ground which is picked up by the grass, causing it to grow, and starting the whole process of like all over again.

From that day on, I had a new appreciation for every lawn in my neighborhood. Grass was no longer merely an outdoor carpet which created fragrant stains on my play clothes. Even during my teenage summers, when I was forced to mow a hot, sweaty acre of grass each weekend before I had a prayer of using the family car on Saturday night, I still retained the respect that Miss Walls had instilled in me years before.

Thanks to her, I still see grass as an amazing mediator between the humans who hurriedly walk over it with their immortal souls and finite lives and the rocks scattered among the blades which seem infinite bad sadly senseless. Like all great teachers, Miss Walls had given my outward eye new sights through fresh insights.

"All flesh is grass," St. Peter said, a thought quite ominous if we only discern the parallel with youth and growth followed by the inevitable mowing down of death. But the organic and cyclical connection between us and the most common growths in nature is comforting as well.

I prefer to see grass as it was presented in the most famous work of literature which mentions grass in its title: Walt Whitman's monumental ***Leaves of Grass***. This seminal volume of poetry is not read much now, but it has recently been made notorious because it seems to have been purchased as a gift by a president for a certain intern. In it, Whitman defines grass as "a handkerchief of the Lord, a scented gift designedly dropped, bearing the Owner's name somewhere in the corner so that we may see, and remark, and say 'whose?'" Not even Charles Dickens could have described grass as brilliantly as being God's monogrammed handkerchief.

The Brazilian Cat

By Arthur Conan Doyle

It is hard luck on a young fellow to have expensive tastes, great expectations, aristocratic connections, but no actual money in his pocket, and no profession by which he may earn any. The fact was that my father, a good, sanguine, easy-going man, had such confidence in the wealth and benevolence of his bachelor elder brother, Lord Southerton, that he took it for granted that I, his only son, would never be called upon to earn a living for myself. He imagined that if there were not a vacancy for me on the great Southerton Estates, at least there would be found some post in that diplomatic service which still remains the special preserve of our privileged classes. He died too early to realize how false his calculations had been. Neither my uncle nor the State took the slightest notice of me, or showed any interest in my career. An occasional brace of pheasants, or basket of hares, was all that ever reached me to remind me that I was heir to Otwell House and one of the richest estates in the country. In the meantime, I found myself a bachelor and man about town, living in a suite of apartments in Grosvenor Mansions, with no occupation save that of pigeon-shooting and polo-playing at Hurlingham. Month by month I realized that it was more and more difficult to get the brokers to renew my bills, or to cash any further post-obits upon an unentailed property. Ruin lay right across my path, and every day I saw it clearer, nearer, and more absolutely unavoidable.

What made me feel my own poverty the more was that, apart from the great wealth of Lord Southerton, all my other relations were fairly well-to-do. The nearest of these was Everard King, my father's nephew and my own first cousin, who had spent an adventurous life in Brazil, and had now returned to this country to settle down on his fortune. We never knew how he made his money, but he appeared to have plenty of it, for he bought the estate of Greylands, near Clipton-on-the-

Marsh, in Suffolk. For the first year of his residence in England he took no more notice of me than my miserly uncle; but at last one summer morning, to my very great relief and joy, I received a letter asking me to come down that very day and spend a short visit at Greylands Court. I was expecting a rather long visit to Bankruptcy Court at the time, and this interruption seemed almost providential. If I could only get on terms with this unknown relative of mine, I might pull through yet. For the family credit he could not let me go entirely to the wall. I ordered my valet to pack my valise, and I set off the same evening for Clipton-on-the-Marsh.

After changing at Ipswich, a little local train deposited me at a small, deserted station lying amidst a rolling grassy country, with a sluggish and winding river curving in and out amidst the valleys, between high, silted banks, which showed that we were within reach of the tide. No carriage was awaiting me (I found afterwards that my telegram had been delayed), so I hired a dogcart at the local inn. The driver, an excellent fellow, was full of my relative's praises, and I learned from him that Mr. Everard King was already a name to conjure with in that part of the county. He had entertained the school-children, he had thrown his grounds open to visitors, he had subscribed to charities--in short, his benevolence had been so universal that my driver could only account for it on the supposition that he had parliamentary ambitions.

My attention was drawn away from my driver's panegyric by the appearance of a very beautiful bird which settled on a telegraph-post beside the road. At first I thought that it was a jay, but it was larger, with a brighter plumage. The driver accounted for its presence at once by saying that it belonged to the very man whom we were about to visit. It seems that the acclimatization of foreign creatures was one of his hobbies, and that he had brought with him from Brazil a number of birds and beasts which he was endeavouring to rear in England. When once we had passed the gates of Greylands Park we had ample evidence of this taste of his. Some small spotted deer, a curious wild pig known, I believe, as a peccary, a gorgeously feathered oriole, some sort of armadillo, and a singular lumbering in-toed beast like a very fat badger, were among the creatures which I observed as we drove along the winding avenue.

Mr. Everard King, my unknown cousin, was standing in person upon the steps of his house, for he had seen us in the distance, and guessed that it was I. His appearance was very homely and benevolent, short and stout, forty-five years old, perhaps, with a round, good-humoured face, burned brown with the tropical sun, and shot with a thousand wrinkles. He wore white linen clothes, in true planter style, with a cigar between his lips, and a large Panama hat upon the back of his head. It was such a figure as one associates with a verandahed bungalow, and it looked curiously out of place in front of this broad, stone English mansion, with its solid wings and its Palladio pillars before the doorway.

"My dear!" he cried, glancing over his shoulder; "my dear, here is our guest! Welcome, welcome to Greylands! I am delighted to make your acquaintance, Cousin Marshall, and I take it as a great compliment that you should honour this sleepy little country place with your presence."

Nothing could be more hearty than his manner, and he set me at my ease in an instant. But it needed all his cordiality to atone for the frigidity and even rudeness of his wife, a tall, haggard woman, who came forward at his summons. She was, I believe, of Brazilian extraction, though she spoke excellent English, and I excused her manners on the score of her ignorance of our customs. She did not attempt to conceal, however, either then or afterwards, that I was no very welcome visitor at Greylands Court. Her actual words were, as a rule, courteous, but she was the possessor of a pair of particularly expressive dark eyes, and I read in them very clearly from the first that she heartily wished me back in London once more.

However, my debts were too pressing and my designs upon my wealthy relative were too vital for me to allow them to be upset by the ill-temper of his wife, so I disregarded her coldness and reciprocated the extreme cordiality of his welcome. No pains had been spared by him to make me comfortable. My room was a charming one. He implored me to tell him anything which could add to my happiness. It was on the tip of my tongue to inform him that a blank cheque would materially help towards that end, but I felt that it might be premature in the present state of our acquaintance. The dinner was excellent, and as we sat together afterwards over his

Havanas and coffee, which later he told me was specially prepared upon his own plantation, it seemed to me that all my driver's eulogies were justified, and that I had never met a more large-hearted and hospitable man.

But, in spite of his cheery good nature, he was a man with a strong will and a fiery temper of his own. Of this I had an example upon the following morning. The curious aversion which Mrs. Everard King had conceived towards me was so strong, that her manner at breakfast was almost offensive. But her meaning became unmistakable when her husband had quitted the room.

"The best train in the day is at twelve-fifteen," said she.

"But I was not thinking of going today," I answered, frankly--perhaps even defiantly, for I was determined not to be driven out by this woman.

"Oh, if it rests with you—" said she, and stopped with a most insolent expression in her eyes.

"I am sure," I answered, "that Mr. Everard King would tell me if I were outstaying my welcome."

"What's this? What's this?" said a voice, and there he was in the room. He had overheard my last words, and a glance at our faces had told him the rest. In an instant his chubby, cheery face set into an expression of absolute ferocity.

"Might I trouble you to walk outside, Marshall?" said he. (I may mention that my own name is Marshall King.)

He closed the door behind me, and then, for an instant, I heard him talking in a low voice of concentrated passion to his wife. This gross breach of hospitality had evidently hit upon his tenderest point. I am no eavesdropper, so I walked out on to the lawn. Presently I heard a hurried step behind me, and there was the lady, her face pale with excitement, and her eyes red with tears.

"My husband has asked me to apologize to you, Mr. Marshall King," said she, standing with downcast eyes before me.

"Please do not say another word, Mrs. King."

Her dark eyes suddenly blazed out at me.

"You fool!" she hissed, with frantic vehemence, and turning on her heel swept back to the house.

The insult was so outrageous, so insufferable, that I could only stand staring after her in bewilderment. I was still there when my host joined me. He was his cheery, chubby self once more.

"I hope that my wife has apologized for her foolish remarks," said he.

"Oh, yes—yes, certainly!"

He put his hand through my arm and walked with me up and down the lawn.

"You must not take it seriously," said he. "It would grieve me inexpressibly if you curtailed your visit by one hour. The fact is—there is no reason why there should be any concealment between relatives—that my poor dear wife is incredibly jealous. She hates that anyone—male or female—should for an instant come between us. Her ideal is a desert island and an eternal tete-a-tete. That gives you the clue to her actions, which are, I confess, upon this particular point, not very far removed from mania. Tell me that you will think no more of it."

"No, no; certainly not."

"Then light this cigar and come round with me and see my little menagerie."

The whole afternoon was occupied by this inspection, which included all the birds, beasts, and even reptiles which he had imported. Some were free, some in cages, a few actually in the house. He spoke with enthusiasm of his successes and his failures, his births and his deaths, and he would cry out in his delight, like a schoolboy, when, as we walked, some gaudy bird would flutter up from the grass, or some curious beast slink into the cover. Finally he led me down a corridor which extended from one wing of the house. At the end of this there was a heavy door with a sliding shutter in it, and beside it there projected from the wall an iron handle attached to a wheel and a drum. A line of stout bars extended across the passage.

"I am about to show you the jewel of my collection," said he. "There is only one other specimen in Europe, now that the Rotterdam cub is dead. It is a Brazilian cat."

"But how does that differ from any other cat?"

"You will soon see that," said he, laughing. "Will you kindly draw that shutter and look through?"

I did so, and found that I was gazing into a large, empty room, with stone flags, and small, barred windows upon the farther wall. In the centre of this room, lying in the middle of a golden patch of sunlight, there was stretched a huge creature, as large as a tiger, but as black and sleek as ebony. It was simply a very enormous and very well-kept black cat, and it cuddled up and basked in that yellow pool of light exactly as a cat would do. It was so graceful, so sinewy, and so gently and smoothly diabolical, that I could not take my eyes from the opening.

"Isn't he splendid?" said my host, enthusiastically.

"Glorious! I never saw such a noble creature."

"Some people call it a black puma, but really it is not a puma at all. That fellow is nearly eleven feet from tail to tip. Four years ago he was a little ball of back fluff, with two yellow eyes staring out of it. He was sold me as a new-born cub up in the wild country at the head-waters of the Rio Negro. They speared his mother to death after she had killed a dozen of them."

"They are ferocious, then?"

"The most absolutely treacherous and bloodthirsty creatures upon earth. You talk about a Brazilian cat to an up-country Indian, and see him get the jumps. They prefer humans to game. This fellow has never tasted living blood yet, but when he does he will be a terror. At present he won't stand anyone but me in his den. Even Baldwin, the groom, dare not go near him. As to me, I am his mother and father in one."

As he spoke he suddenly, to my astonishment, opened the door and slipped in, closing it instantly behind him. At the sound of his voice the huge, lithe creature rose, yawned and rubbed its round, black head affectionately against his side, while he patted and fondled it.

"Now, Tommy, into your cage!" said he.

The monstrous cat walked over to one side of the room and coiled itself up under a grating. Everard King came out, and taking the iron handle which I have mentioned, he began to turn it. As he did so the line of bars in the corridor began to pass through a slot in the wall and closed up the front of this grating, so as to make an effective cage. When it was in position he opened the door once more and invited me into the room, which was heavy with the pungent, musty smell peculiar to the great carnivora.

"That's how we work it," said he. "We give him the run of the room for exercise, and then at night we put him in his cage. You can let him out by turning the handle from the passage, or you can, as you have seen, coop him up in the same way. No, no, you should not do that!"

I had put my hand between the bars to pat the glossy, heaving flank. He pulled it back, with a serious face.

"I assure you that he is not safe. Don't imagine that because I can take liberties with him anyone else can. He is very exclusive in his friends—aren't you, Tommy? Ah, he hears his lunch coming to him! Don't you, boy?"

A step sounded in the stone-flagged passage, and the creature had sprung to his feet, and was pacing up and down the narrow cage, his yellow eyes gleaming, and his scarlet tongue rippling and quivering over the white line of his jagged teeth. A groom entered with a coarse joint upon a tray, and thrust it through the bars to him. He pounced lightly upon it, carried it off to the corner, and there, holding it between his paws, tore and wrenched at it, raising his bloody muzzle every now and then to look at us. It was a malignant and yet fascinating sight.

"You can't wonder that I am fond of him, can you?" said my host, as we left the room, "especially when you consider that I have had the rearing of him. It was no joke bringing him over from the centre of South America; but here he is safe and sound—and, as I have said, far the most perfect specimen in Europe. The people at the Zoo are dying to have him, but I really can't part with him. Now, I think that I have inflicted my hobby upon you long enough, so we cannot do better than follow Tommy's example, and go to our lunch."

My South American relative was so engrossed by his grounds and their curious occupants, that I hardly gave him credit at first for having any interests outside them. That he had some, and pressing ones, was soon borne in upon me by the number of telegrams which he received. They arrived at all hours, and were always opened by him with the utmost eagerness and anxiety upon his face. Sometimes I imagined that it must be the Turf, and sometimes the Stock Exchange, but certainly he had some very urgent business going forwards which was not transacted upon the Downs of Suffolk. During the six days of my visit he had never fewer than three or four telegrams a day, and sometimes as many as seven or eight.

I had occupied these six days so well, that by the end of them I had succeeded in getting upon the most cordial terms with my cousin. Every night we had sat up late in the billiard-room, he telling me the most extraordinary stories of his adventures in America—stories so desperate and reckless, that I could hardly associate them with the brown little, chubby man before me. In return, I ventured upon some of my own reminiscences of London life, which interested him so much, that he vowed he would come up to Grosvenor Mansions and stay with me. He was anxious to see the faster side of city life, and certainly, though I say it, he could not have chosen a more competent guide. It was not until the last day of my visit that I ventured to approach that which was on my mind. I told him frankly about my pecuniary difficulties and my impending ruin, and I asked his advice—though I hoped for something more solid. He listened attentively, puffing hard at his cigar.

"But surely," said he, "you are the heir of our relative, Lord Southerton?"

"I have every reason to believe so, but he would never make me any allowance."

"No, no, I have heard of his miserly ways. My poor Marshall, your position has been a very hard one. By the way, have you heard any news of Lord Southerton's health lately?"

"He has always been in a critical condition ever since my childhood."

"Exactly—a creaking hinge, if ever there was one. Your inheritance may be a long way off. Dear me, how awkwardly situated you are!"

"I had some hopes, sir, that you, knowing all the facts, might be inclined to advance--"

"Don't say another word, my dear boy," he cried, with the utmost cordiality; "we shall talk it over tonight, and I give you my word that whatever is in my power shall be done."

I was not sorry that my visit was drawing to a close, for it is unpleasant to feel that there is one person in the house who eagerly desires your departure. Mrs. King's sallow face and forbidding eyes had become more and more hateful to me. She was no longer actively rude—her fear of her husband prevented her—but she pushed her insane jealousy to the extent of ignoring me, never addressing me, and in every way making my stay at Greylands as uncomfortable as she could. So offensive was her manner during that last day, that I should certainly have left had it not been for that interview with my host in the evening which would, I hoped, retrieve my broken fortunes.

It was very late when it occurred, for my relative, who had been receiving even more telegrams than usual during the day, went off to his study after dinner, and only emerged when the household had retired to bed. I heard him go round locking the doors, as custom was of a night, and finally he joined me in the billiard-room. His stout figure was wrapped in a dressing-gown, and he wore a pair of red Turkish slippers without any heels. Settling down into an armchair, he brewed himself a glass of grog, in which I could not help noticing that the whisky considerably predominated over the water.

"My word!" said he, "what a night!"

It was, indeed. The wind was howling and screaming round the house, and the latticed windows rattled and shook as if they were coming in. The glow of the yellow lamps and the flavour of our cigars seemed the brighter and more fragrant for the contrast.

"Now, my boy," said my host, "we have the house and the night to ourselves. Let me have an idea of how your affairs stand, and I will see what can be done to set them in order. I wish to hear every detail."

Thus encouraged, I entered into a long exposition, in which all my tradesmen and creditors from my landlord to my valet, figured in turn. I had notes in my pocketbook, and I marshaled my facts, and gave, I flatter myself, a very businesslike statement of my own unbusinesslike ways and lamentable position. I was depressed, however, to notice that my companion's eyes were vacant and his attention elsewhere. When he did occasionally throw out a remark it was so entirely perfunctory and pointless, that I was sure he had not in the least followed my remarks. Every now and then he roused himself and put on some show of interest, asking me to repeat or to explain more fully, but it was always to sink once more into the same brown study. At last he rose and threw the end of his cigar into the grate.

"I'll tell you what, my boy," said he. "I never had a head for figures, so you will excuse me. You must jot it all down upon paper, and let me have a note of the amount. I'll understand it when I see it in black and white."

The proposal was encouraging. I promised to do so.

"And now it's time we were in bed. By Jove, there's one o'clock striking in the hall."

The tingling of the chiming clock broke through the deep roar of the gale. The wind was sweeping past with the rush of a great river.

"I must see my cat before I go to bed," said my host. "A high wind excites him. Will you come?"

"Certainly," said I.

"Then tread softly and don't speak, for everyone is asleep."

We passed quietly down the lamp-lit Persian-rugged hall, and through the door at the farther end. All was dark in the stone corridor, but a stable lantern hung on a hook, and my host took it down and lit it. There was no grating visible in the passage, so I knew that the beast was in its cage.

"Come in!" said my relative, and opened the door.

A deep growling as we entered showed that the storm had really excited the creature. In the flickering light of the lantern, we saw it, a huge black mass coiled in the corner of its den and throwing a squat, uncouth shadow upon the whitewashed wall. Its tail switched angrily among the straw.

"Poor Tommy is not in the best of tempers," said Everard King, holding up the lantern and looking in at him. "What a black devil he looks, doesn't he? I must give him a little supper to put him in a better humour. Would you mind holding the lantern for a moment?"

I took it from his hand and he stepped to the door.

"His larder is just outside here," said he. "You will excuse me for an instant won't you?" He passed out, and the door shut with a sharp metallic click behind him.

That hard crisp sound made my heart stand still. A sudden wave of terror passed over me. A vague perception of some monstrous treachery turned me cold. I sprang to the door, but there was no handle upon the inner side.

76

"Here!" I cried. "Let me out!"

"All right! Don't make a row!" said my host from the passage. "You've got the light all right."

"Yes, but I don't care about being locked in alone like this."

"Don't you?" I heard his hearty, chuckling laugh. "You won't be alone long."

"Let me out, sir!" I repeated angrily. "I tell you I don't allow practical jokes of this sort."

"Practical is the word," said he, with another hateful chuckle. And then suddenly I heard, amidst the roar of the storm, the creak and whine of the winch-handle turning and the rattle of the grating as it passed through the slot. Great God, he was letting loose the Brazilian cat!

In the light of the lantern I saw the bars sliding slowly before me. Already there was an opening a foot wide at the farther end. With a scream I seized the last bar with my hands and pulled with the strength of a madman. I WAS a madman with rage and horror. For a minute or more I held the thing motionless. I knew that he was straining with all his force upon the handle, and that the leverage was sure to overcome me. I gave inch by inch, my feet sliding along the stones, and all the time I begged and prayed this inhuman monster to save me from this horrible death. I conjured him by his kinship. I reminded him that I was his guest; I begged to know what harm I had ever done him. His only answers were the tugs and jerks upon the handle, each of which, in spite of all my struggles, pulled another bar through the opening. Clinging and clutching, I was dragged across the whole front of the cage, until at last, with aching wrists and lacerated fingers, I gave up the hopeless struggle. The grating clanged back as I released it, and an instant later I heard the shuffle of the Turkish slippers in the passage, and the slam of the distant door. Then everything was silent.

The creature had never moved during this time. He lay still in the corner, and his tail had ceased switching. This apparition of a man adhering to his bars and dragged screaming across him had apparently filled him with amazement. I saw his great eyes staring steadily at me. I had dropped the lantern when I seized the bars, but it still burned upon the floor, and I made a movement to grasp it, with some idea that its light might protect me. But the instant I moved, the beast gave a deep and menacing growl. I stopped and stood still, quivering with fear in every limb. The cat (if one may call so fearful a creature by so homely a name) was not more than ten feet from me. The eyes glimmered like two disks of phosphorus in the darkness. They appalled and yet fascinated me. I could not take my own eyes from them. Nature plays strange tricks with us at such moments of intensity, and those glimmering lights waxed and waned with a steady rise and fall. Sometimes they seemed to be tiny points of extreme brilliancy—little electric sparks in the black obscurity—then they would widen and widen until all that corner of the room was filled with their shifting and sinister light. And then suddenly they went out altogether.

The beast had closed its eyes. I do not know whether there may be any truth in the old idea of the dominance of the human gaze, or whether the huge cat was simply drowsy, but the fact remains that, far from showing any symptom of attacking me, it simply rested its sleek, black head upon its huge forepaws and seemed to sleep. I stood, fearing to move lest I should rouse it into malignant life once more. But at least I was able to think clearly now that the baleful eyes were off me. Here I was shut up for the night with the ferocious beast. My own instincts, to say nothing of the words of the plausible villain who laid this trap for me, warned me that the animal was as savage as its master. How could I stave it off until morning? The door was hopeless, and so were the narrow, barred windows. There was no shelter anywhere in the bare, stone-flagged room. To cry for assistance was absurd. I knew that this den was an outhouse, and that the corridor which connected it with the house was at least a hundred feet long. Besides, with the gale thundering outside, my cries were not likely to be heard. I had only my own courage and my own wits to trust to.

And then, with a fresh wave of horror, my eyes fell upon the lantern. The candle had burned low, and was already beginning to gutter. In ten minutes it would be out. I had only ten minutes then in which to do something, for I felt that if I were once left in the dark with that fearful beast I should be incapable of action. The very thought of it paralyzed me. I cast my despairing eyes round this chamber of death, and they rested upon one spot which seemed to promise I will not say safety, but less immediate and imminent danger than the open floor.

I have said that the cage had a top as well as a front, and this top was left standing when the front was wound through the slot in the wall. It consisted of bars at a few inches' interval, with stout wire netting between, and it rested upon a strong stanchion at each end. It stood now as a great barred canopy over the crouching figure in the corner. The space between this iron shelf and the roof may have been from two or three feet. If I could only get up there, squeezed in between bars and ceiling, I should have only one vulnerable side. I should be safe from below, from behind, and from each side. Only on the open face of it could I be attacked. There, it is true, I had no protection whatever; but at least, I should be out of the brute's path when he began to pace about his den. He would have to come out of his way to reach me. It was now or never, for if once the light were out it would be impossible. With a gulp in my throat I sprang up, seized the iron edge of the top, and swung myself panting on to it. I writhed in face downwards, and found myself looking straight into the terrible eyes and yawning jaws of the cat. Its fetid breath came up into my face like the steam from some foul pot.

It appeared, however, to be rather curious than angry. With a sleek ripple of its long, black back it rose, stretched itself, and then rearing itself on its hind legs, with one forepaw against the wall, it raised the other, and drew its claws across the wire meshes beneath me. One sharp, white hook tore through my trousers—for I may mention that I was still in evening dress—and dug a furrow in my knee. It was not meant as an attack, but rather as an experiment, for upon my giving a sharp cry of pain he dropped down again, and springing lightly into the room, he began walking swiftly round it, looking up every now and again in my direction. For my part I shuffled backwards until I lay with my back against the wall, screwing myself into the smallest space possible. The farther I got the more difficult it was for him to attack me.

He seemed more excited now that he had begun to move about, and he ran swiftly and noiselessly round and round the den, passing continually underneath the iron couch upon which

I lay. It was wonderful to see so great a bulk passing like a shadow, with hardly the softest thudding of velvety pads. The candle was burning low—so low that I could hardly see the creature. And then, with a last flare and splutter it went out altogether. I was alone with the cat in the dark!

It helps one to face a danger when one knows that one has done all that possibly can be done. There is nothing for it then but to quietly await the result. In this case, there was no chance of safety anywhere except the precise spot where I was. I stretched myself out, therefore, and lay silently, almost breathlessly, hoping that the beast might forget my presence if I did nothing to remind him. I reckoned that it must already be two o'clock. At four it would be full dawn. I had not more than two hours to wait for daylight.

Outside, the storm was still raging, and the rain lashed continually against the little windows. Inside, the poisonous and fetid air was overpowering. I could neither hear nor see the cat. I tried to think about other things—but only one had power enough to draw my mind from my terrible position. That was the contemplation of my cousin's villainy, his unparalleled hypocrisy, his malignant hatred of me. Beneath that cheerful face there lurked the spirit of a mediaeval assassin. And as I thought of it I saw more clearly how cunningly the thing had been arranged. He had apparently gone to bed with the others. No doubt he had his witness to prove it. Then, unknown to them, he had slipped down, had lured me into his den and abandoned me. His story would be so simple. He had left me to finish my cigar in the billiard-room. I had gone down on my own account to have a last look at the cat. I had entered the room without observing that the cage was opened, and I had been caught. How could such a crime be brought home to him? Suspicion, perhaps—but proof, never!

How slowly those dreadful two hours went by! Once I heard a low, rasping sound, which I took to be the creature licking its own fur. Several times those greenish eyes gleamed at me through the darkness, but never in a fixed stare, and my hopes grew stronger that my presence had been forgotten or ignored. At last the least faint glimmer of light came through the windows—I first dimly saw them as two grey squares upon the black wall, then grey turned to white, and I could see my terrible companion once more. And he, alas, could see me!

It was evident to me at once that he was in a much more dangerous and aggressive mood than when I had seen him last. The cold of the morning had irritated him, and he was hungry as well. With a continual growl he paced swiftly up and down the side of the room which was farthest from my refuge, his whiskers bristling angrily, and his tail switching and lashing. As he turned at the corners his savage eyes always looked upwards at me with a dreadful menace. I knew then that he meant to kill me. Yet I found myself even at that moment admiring the sinuous grace of the devilish thing, its long, undulating, rippling movements, the gloss of its beautiful flanks, the vivid, palpitating scarlet of the glistening tongue which hung from the jet-black muzzle. And all the time that deep, threatening growl was rising and rising in an unbroken crescendo. I knew that the crisis was at hand.

It was a miserable hour to meet such a death—so cold, so comfortless, shivering in my light dress clothes upon this gridiron of torment upon which I was stretched. I tried to brace myself to it, to raise my soul above it, and at the same time, with the lucidity which comes to a perfectly desperate man, I cast round for some possible means of escape. One thing was clear to me. If that front of the cage was only back in its position once more, I could find a sure refuge behind it. Could I possibly pull it back? I hardly dared to move for fear of bringing the creature upon me. Slowly, very slowly, I put my hand forward until it grasped the edge of the front, the final bar which protruded through the wall. To my surprise it came quite easily to my jerk. Of course the difficulty of drawing it out arose from the fact that I was clinging to it. I pulled again, and three inches of it came through. It ran apparently on wheels. I pulled again ... and then the cat sprang!

It was so quick, so sudden, that I never saw it happen. I simply heard the savage snarl, and in an instant afterwards the blazing yellow eyes, the flattened black head with its red tongue and flashing teeth, were within reach of me. The impact of the creature shook the bars upon which I lay, until I thought (as far as I could think of anything at such a moment) that they were coming down. The cat swayed there for an instant, the head and front paws quite close to me, the hind paws clawing to find a grip upon the edge of the grating. I heard the claws rasping as they clung to the wire-netting, and the breath of the beast made me sick. But its bound had been miscalculated. It could not retain its position. Slowly, grinning with rage, and scratching madly at the bars, it swung backwards and dropped heavily upon the floor. With a growl it instantly faced round to me and crouched for another spring.

I knew that the next few moments would decide my fate. The creature had learned by experience. It would not miscalculate again. I must act promptly, fearlessly, if I were to have a chance for life. In an instant I had formed my plan. Pulling off my dress-coat, I threw it down over the head of the beast. At the same moment I dropped over the edge, seized the end of the front grating, and pulled it frantically out of the wall.

It came more easily than I could have expected. I rushed across the room, bearing it with me; but, as I rushed, the accident of my position put me upon the outer side. Had it been the other way, I might have come off scathless. As it was, there was a moment's pause as I stopped it and tried to pass in through the opening which I had left. That moment was enough to give time to the creature to toss off the coat with which I had blinded him and to spring upon me. I hurled myself through the gap and pulled the rails to behind me, but he seized my leg before I could entirely withdraw it. One stroke of that huge paw tore off my calf as a shaving of wood curls off before a plane. The next moment, bleeding and fainting, I was lying among the foul straw with a line of friendly bars between me and the creature which ramped so frantically against them.

Too wounded to move, and too faint to be conscious of fear, I could only lie, more dead than alive, and watch it. It pressed its broad, black chest against the bars and angled for me with its crooked paws as I have seen a kitten do before a mousetrap. It ripped my clothes, but, stretch as it would, it could not quite reach me. I have heard of the curious numbing effect produced by wounds from the great carnivora, and now I was destined to experience it, for I had lost all sense of personality, and was as interested in the cat's failure or success as if it were some game which I was watching. And then gradually my mind drifted away into strange vague dreams, always with that black face and red tongue coming back into them, and so I lost myself in the nirvana of delirium, the blessed relief of those who are too sorely tried.

Tracing the course of events afterwards, I conclude that I must have been insensible for about two hours. What roused me to consciousness once more was that sharp metallic click which had been the precursor of my terrible experience. It was the shooting back of the spring lock. Then, before my senses were clear enough to entirely apprehend what they saw, I was aware of the round, benevolent face of my cousin peering in through the open door. What he saw evidently amazed him. There was the cat crouching on the floor. I was stretched upon my back in my shirt-sleeves within the cage, my trousers torn to ribbons and a great pool of blood all round me. I can see his amazed face now, with the morning sunlight upon it. He peered at me, and peered again. Then he closed the door behind him, and advanced to the cage to see if I were really dead.

I cannot undertake to say what happened. I was not in a fit state to witness or to chronicle such events. I can only say that I was suddenly conscious that his face was away from me—that he was looking towards the animal.

"Good old Tommy!" he cried. "Good old Tommy!"

Then he came near the bars, with his back still towards me.

"Down, you stupid beast!" he roared. "Down, sir! Don't you know your master?"

Suddenly even in my bemuddled brain a remembrance came of those words of his when he had said that the taste of blood would turn the cat into a fiend. My blood had done it, but he was to pay the price.

"Get away!" he screamed. "Get away, you devil! Baldwin! Baldwin! Oh, my God!"

And then I heard him fall, and rise, and fall again, with a sound like the ripping of sacking. His screams grew fainter until they were lost in the worrying snarl. And then, after I thought that he was dead, I saw, as in a nightmare, a blinded, tattered, blood-soaked figure running wildly round the room—and that was the last glimpse which I had of him before I fainted once again.

I was many months in my recovery—in fact, I cannot say that I have ever recovered, for to the end of my days I shall carry a stick as a sign of my night with the Brazilian cat. Baldwin, the groom, and the other servants could not tell what had occurred, when, drawn by the death-cries of their master, they found me behind the bars, and his remains—or what they afterwards discovered to be his remains—in the clutch of the creature which he had reared. They stalled him off with hot irons, and afterwards shot him through the loophole of the door before they could finally extricate me. I was carried to my bedroom, and there, under the roof of my would-be murderer, I remained between life and death for several weeks. They had sent for a surgeon from Clipton and a nurse from London, and in a month I was able to be carried to the station, and so conveyed back once more to Grosvenor Mansions.

I have one remembrance of that illness, which might have been part of the ever-changing panorama conjured up by a delirious brain were it not so definitely fixed in my memory. One night, when the nurse was absent, the door of my chamber opened, and a tall woman in blackest mourning slipped into the room. She came across to me, and as she bent her sallow face I saw by the faint gleam of the nightlight that it was the Brazilian woman whom my cousin had married. She stared intently into my face, and her expression was more kindly than I had ever seen it.

"Are you conscious?" she asked.

I feebly nodded—for I was still very weak.

"Well; then, I only wished to say to you that you have yourself to blame. Did I not do all I could for you? From the beginning I tried to drive you from the house. By every means, short of betraying my husband, I tried to save you from him. I knew that he had a reason for bringing you here. I knew that he would never let you get away again. No one knew him as I knew him, who had suffered from him so often. I did not dare to tell you all this. He would have killed me. But I did my best for you. As things have turned out, you have been the best friend that I have ever had. You have set me free, and I fancied that nothing but death would do that. I am sorry if you are hurt, but I cannot reproach myself. I told you that you were a fool—and a fool you have been." She crept out of the room, the bitter, singular woman, and I was never destined to see her again.

With what remained from her husband's property she went back to her native land, and I have heard that she afterwards took the veil at Pernambuco.

It was not until I had been back in London for some time that the doctors pronounced me to be well enough to do business. It was not a very welcome permission to me, for I feared that it would be the signal for an inrush of creditors; but it was Summers, my lawyer, who first took advantage of it.

"I am very glad to see that your lordship is so much better," said he. "I have been waiting a long time to offer my congratulations."

"What do you mean, Summers? This is no time for joking."

"I mean what I say," he answered. "You have been Lord Southerton for the last six weeks, but we feared that it would retard your recovery if you were to learn it."

Lord Southerton! One of the richest peers in England! I could not believe my ears. And then suddenly I thought of the time which had elapsed, and how it coincided with my injuries.

"Then Lord Southerton must have died about the same time that I was hurt?"

"His death occurred upon that very day." Summers looked hard at me as I spoke, and I am convinced—for he was a very shrewd fellow—that he had guessed the true state of the case. He paused for a moment as if awaiting a confidence from me, but I could not see what was to be gained by exposing such a family scandal.

"Yes, a very curious coincidence," he continued, with the same knowing look. "Of course, you are aware that your cousin Everard King was the next heir to the estates. Now, if it had been you instead of him who had been torn to pieces by this tiger, or whatever it was, then of course he would have been Lord Southerton at the present moment."

"No doubt," said I.

"And he took such an interest in it," said Summers. "I happen to know that the late Lord Southerton's valet was in his pay, and that he used to have telegrams from him every few hours to tell him how he was getting on. That would be about the time when you were down there. Was it not strange that he should wish to be so well informed, since he knew that he was not the direct heir?"

"Very strange," said I. "And now, Summers, if you will bring me my bills and a new cheque-book, we will begin to get things into order."

The cat remains the friend of man because it pleases him to do so and not because he must. --- Carl Van Vechten

Dog

Canine

BowWow

Cur

Fido

Flea Bag

Hound

Man's Best Friend

Doggy

Mongrel

Mutt

Pooch

Pup

Puppy

Stray

Tail-Wagger

Tyke

> *All three of these stories emphasize the bond between a dog and its master but it is the emphasis on master, dog, and **alcohol** in the O. Henry story that makes my essay appropriate here.*

Dickens considered *David Copperfield* his favorite novel, and most critics believe the earlier chapters, detailing David's childhood and youth, to be the finest. I personally find Chapter Twenty-four, which contains David's account of the first time he became drunk, especially delightful, perhaps because it makes me recall my own youthful pathetic attempt at intoxication.

My total consumption of liquor in high school would not have registered a .0004 on a breathalyzer. I decided to remedy this situation shortly before graduation, on a Friday night when my parents were out for the evening. I was limited as to choice of liquor since my mother and father would have a drink only in a restaurant on a very special occasion. Our home "bar," therefore, consisted of one ancient bottle each of scotch, cherry brandy, and vodka kept in a corner cupboard and trotted out only when requested by a guest.

I decided on the vodka since it looked and smelled as innocent as water. The label was so faded and the cap so sticky tight that I feared the last time the bottle had been opened was to celebrate my birth. Since I still had a passion for chocolate milk, I wondered if a concoction of half vodka and half chocolate milk might be the sweetest way to achieve intoxication.

I downed an enormous amount of the gruesome brew in an astonishingly short period of time; I upped the same amount followed by my earlier dinner, lunch, and breakfast in no particular order but at frequent intervals over the next two hours. I never understood until that night why miserable people were called *wretches*. My introduction to booze had quickly become an introduction to bulimia. For this kind of entertainment, I could have skipped the vodka and simply swallowed some paregoric.

Nauseated and dizzy, I decided that drinking alone was indeed a sad experience. Rather desperate for a drinking buddy on short notice, I shakily poured a bit of the liquored milk into my dog Bobo's water bowl. She sniffed it suspiciously, gazed up at me with a disappointed stare, and then walked off, her indication that the term "dumb animal" should occasionally be applied to the owner.

After all my retching, I barely had enough strength to clean up the considerable mess in both kitchen and bathroom. First, I refilled the vodka bottle with water, figuring that even if my parents did imbibe at some distant date their inexperience with drinking would keep them none the wiser. I then scrubbed and deodorized with an energy and thoroughness that would have amazed my mother, had I been able to share with her my cleaning frenzy. But I feared the punishment which would await me if she or my father discovered my abortive binge. Finally, I crawled into bed, sick but secure in the knowledge that the kitchen counters and bathroom facilities were as spotless as when my parents left hours before. Who says that a drunk can't successfully cover his tracks?

I say. I awoke the next morning with a throbbing head, soon to be followed by a throbbing rear-end after my mother greeted my wobbly arrival in the kitchen with one pressing (and depressing) question: "How in the world did fermented chocolate milk get into Bobo's water bowl?" I was foiled by Fido, man's best friend, perhaps, but a teetotaler traitor to his teenaged master.

Memoirs of a Yellow Dog

By O. Henry

I don't suppose it will knock any of you people off your perch to read a contribution from an animal. Mr. Kipling and a good many others have demonstrated the fact that animals can express themselves in remunerative English, and no magazine goes to press nowadays without an animal story in it, except the old-style monthlies that are still running pictures of Bryan and the Mont Pelee horror.

But you needn't look for any stuck-up literature in my piece, such as Bearoo, the bear, and Snakoo, the snake, and Tammanoo, the tiger, talk in the jungle books. A yellow dog that's spent most of his life in a cheap New York flat, sleeping in a corner on an old sateen underskirt (the one she spilled port wine on at the Lady Longshoremen's banquet), mustn't be expected to perform any tricks with the art of speech.

I was born a yellow pup; date, locality, pedigree and weight unknown. The first thing I can recollect, an old woman had me in a basket at Broadway and Twenty-third trying to sell me to a fat lady. Old Mother Hubbard was boosting me to beat the band as a genuine Pomeranian-Hambletonian-Red-Irish-Cochin-China-Stoke-Pogis fox terrier. The fat lady chased a V around among the samples of gros grain flannelette in her shopping bag till she cornered it, and gave up. From that moment I was a pet—a mamma's own wootsey squidlums. Say, gentle reader, did you ever have a 200-pound woman breathing a flavour of Camembert cheese and Peau d'Espagne pick you up and wallop her nose all over you, remarking all the time in an Emma Eames tone of voice: "Oh, oo's um oodlum, doodlum, woodlum, toodlum, bitsy-witsy skoodlums?"

From a pedigreed yellow pup I grew up to be an anonymous yellow cur looking like a cross between an Angora cat and a box of lemons. But my mistress never tumbled. She thought that the two primeval pups that Noah chased into the ark were but a collateral branch of my ancestors. It took two policemen to keep her from entering me at the Madison Square Garden for the Siberian bloodhound prize.

I'll tell you about that flat. The house was the ordinary thing in New York, paved with Parian marble in the entrance hall and cobblestones above the first floor. Our flat was three—well, not flights—climbs up. My mistress rented it unfurnished, and put in the regular things—1903 antique upholstered parlour set, oil chromo of geishas in a Harlem tea house, rubber plant and husband.

By Sirius! there was a biped I felt sorry for. He was a little man with sandy hair and whiskers a good deal like mine. Henpecked?—well, toucans and flamingoes and pelicans all had their bills in him. He wiped the dishes and listened to my mistress tell about the cheap, ragged things the lady with the squirrel-skin coat on the second floor hung out on her line to dry. And every evening while she was getting supper she made him take me out on the end of a string for a walk.

If men knew how women pass the time when they are alone they'd never marry. Laura Lean Jibbey, peanut brittle, a little almond cream on the neck muscles, dishes unwashed, half an hour's talk with the iceman, reading a package of old letters, a couple of pickles and two bottles of malt extract, one hour peeking through a hole in the window shade into the flat across the airshaft—that's about all there is to it. Twenty minutes before time for him to come home from work she straightens up the house, fixes her rat so it won't show, and gets out a lot of sewing for a ten-minute bluff.

I led a dog's life in that flat. 'Most all day I lay there in my corner watching that fat woman kill time. I slept sometimes and had pipe dreams about being out chasing cats into basements and growling at old ladies with black mittens, as a dog was intended to do. Then she would pounce upon me with a lot of that driveling poodle palaver and kiss me on the nose—but what could I do? A dog can't chew gloves.

I began to feel sorry for Hubby, dog my cats if I didn't. We looked so much alike that people noticed it when we went out; so we shook the streets that Morgan's cab drives down, and took to climbing the piles of last December's snow on the streets where cheap people live.

One evening when we were thus promenading, and I was trying to look like a prize St. Bernard, and the old man was trying to look like he wouldn't have murdered the first organ-grinder he heard play Mendelssohn's wedding-march, I looked up at him and said, in my way:

"What are you looking so sour about, you oakum trimmed lobster? She don't kiss you. You don't have to sit on her lap and listen to talk that would make the book of a musical comedy sound like the maxims of Epictetus. You ought to be thankful you're not a dog. Brace up, Benedick, and bid the blues begone."

The matrimonial mishap looked down at me with almost canine intelligence in his face.

"Why, doggie," says he, "good doggie. You almost look like you could speak. What is it, doggie—Cats?"

Cats! Could speak!

But, of course, he couldn't understand. Humans were denied the speech of animals. The only common ground of communication upon which dogs and men can get together is in fiction.

In the flat across the hall from us lived a lady with a black-and-tan terrier. Her husband strung it and took it out every evening, but he always came home cheerful and whistling. One day I touched noses with the black-and-tan in the hall, and I struck him for an elucidation.

"See, here, Wiggle-and-Skip," I says, "you know that it ain't the nature of a real man to play dry nurse to a dog in public. I never saw one leashed to a bow-wow yet that didn't look like he'd like to lick every other man that looked at him. But your boss comes in every day as perky and set up as an amateur prestidigitator doing the egg trick. How does he do it? Don't tell me he likes it."

"Him?" says the black-and-tan. "Why, he uses Nature's Own Remedy. He gets spifflicated. At first when we go out he's as shy as the man on the steamer who would rather play Pedro when they make 'em all jackpots. By the time we've been in eight saloons he don't care whether the thing on the end of his line is a dog or a catfish. I've lost two inches of my tail trying to sidestep those swinging doors."

The pointer I got from that terrier—vaudeville please copy—set me to thinking.

One evening about 6 o'clock my mistress ordered him to get busy and do the ozone act for Lovey. I have concealed it until now, but that is what she called me. The black-and-tan was called "Tweetness." I consider that I have the bulge on him as far as you could chase a rabbit. Still "Lovey" is something of a nomenclatural tin can on the tail of one's self respect.

At a quiet place on a safe street I tightened the line of my custodian in front of an attractive, refined saloon. I made a dead-ahead scramble for the doors, whining like a dog in the press dispatches that lets the family know that little Alice is bogged while gathering lilies in the brook.

"Why, darn my eyes," says the old man, with a grin; "darn my eyes if the saffron-coloured son of a seltzer lemonade ain't asking me in to take a drink. Lemme see—how long's it been since I saved shoe leather by keeping one foot on the footrest? I believe I'll--"

I knew I had him. Hot Scotches he took, sitting at a table. For an hour he kept the Campbells coming. I sat by his side rapping for the waiter with my tail, and eating free lunch such as mamma in her flat never equalled with her homemade truck bought at a delicatessen store eight minutes before papa comes home.

When the products of Scotland were all exhausted except the rye bread the old man unwound me from the table leg and played me outside like a fisherman plays a salmon. Out there he took off my collar and threw it into the street.

"Poor doggie," says he; "good doggie. She shan't kiss you anymore. 'S a darned shame. Good doggie, go away and get run over by a street car and be happy."

I refused to leave. I leaped and frisked around the old man's legs happy as a pug on a rug.

"You old flea-headed woodchuck-chaser," I said to him—" you moon-baying, rabbit-pointing, egg-stealing old beagle, can't you see that I don't want to leave you? Can't you see that we're both Pups in the Wood and the missis is the cruel uncle after you with the dish towel and me with the flea liniment and a pink bow to tie on my tail. Why not cut that all out and be pards forever more?"

Maybe you'll say he didn't understand—maybe he didn't. But he kind of got a grip on the Hot Scotches, and stood still for a minute, thinking.

"Doggie," says he, finally, "we don't live more than a dozen lives on this earth, and very few of us live to be more than 300. If I ever see that flat any more I'm a flat, and if you do you're flatter; and that's no flattery. I'm offering 60 to 1 that Westward Ho wins out by the length of a dachshund."

There was no string, but I frolicked along with my master to the Twenty-third street ferry. And the cats on the route saw reason to give thanks that prehensile claws had been given them.

On the Jersey side my master said to a stranger who stood eating a currant bun:

"Me and my doggie, we are bound for the Rocky Mountains."

But what pleased me most was when my old man pulled both of my ears until I howled, and said:

"You common, monkey-headed, rat-tailed, sulphur-coloured son of a door mat, do you know what I'm going to call you?"

I thought of "Lovey," and I whined dolefully.

"I'm going to call you 'Pete,'" says my master; and if I'd had five tails I couldn't have done enough wagging to do justice to the occasion.

The Dog

By Ivan Turgenev

Translated From The Russian
By Isabel Hapgood

There are two of us in the room, my dog and I.... A frightful storm is raging out of doors.

The dog is sitting in front of me, and gazing straight into my eyes.

And I, also, am looking him straight in the eye.

He seems to be anxious to say something to me. He is dumb, he has no words, he does not understand himself—but I understand him.

I understand that, at this moment, both in him and in me there dwells one and the same feeling, that there is no difference whatever between us. We are exactly alike; in each of us there burns and glows the selfsame tremulous flame.

Death is swooping down upon us, it is waving its cold, broad wings....

"And this is the end!"

Who shall decide afterward, precisely what sort of flame burned in each one of us?

No! it is not an animal and a man exchanging glances....

It is two pairs of eyes exactly alike fixed on each other.

And in each of those pairs, in the animal and in the man, one and the same life is huddling up timorously to the other.

The Tinder Box

By Hans Christian Andersen

A soldier came marching along the high road: "Left, right—left, right." He had his knapsack on his back, and a sword at his side; he had been to the wars, and was now returning home.

As he walked on, he met a very frightful-looking old witch in the road. Her under-lip hung quite down on her breast, and she stopped and said, "Good evening, soldier; you have a very fine sword, and a large knapsack, and you are a real soldier; so you shall have as much money as ever you like."

"Thank you, old witch," said the soldier.

"Do you see that large tree," said the witch, pointing to a tree which stood beside them. "Well, it is quite hollow inside, and you must climb to the top, when you will see a hole, through which you can let yourself down into the tree to a great depth. I will tie a rope round your body, so that I can pull you up again when you call out to me."

"But what am I to do, down there in the tree?" asked the soldier.

"Get money," she replied; "for you must know that when you reach the ground under the tree, you will find yourself in a large hall, lighted up by three hundred lamps; you will then see three doors, which can be easily opened, for the keys are in all the locks. On entering the first of the chambers, to which these doors lead, you will see a large chest, standing in the middle of the floor, and upon it a dog seated, with a pair of eyes as large as teacups. But you need not be at all afraid of him; I will give you my blue checked apron, which you must spread upon the floor, and then boldly seize hold of the dog, and place him upon it. You can then open the chest, and take from it as many pence as you please, they are only copper pence; but if you would rather have silver money, you must go into the second chamber. Here you will find another dog, with eyes as big as mill-wheels;

but do not let that trouble you. Place him upon my apron, and then take what money you please. If, however, you like gold best, enter the third chamber, where there is another chest full of it. The dog who sits on this chest is very dreadful; his eyes are as big as a tower, but do not mind him. If he also is placed upon my apron, he cannot hurt you, and you may take from the chest what gold you will."

"This is not a bad story," said the soldier; "but what am I to give you, you old witch? For, of course, you do not mean to tell me all this for nothing."

"No," said the witch; "but I do not ask for a single penny. Only promise to bring me an old tinderbox, which my grandmother left behind the last time she went down there."

"Very well; I promise. Now tie the rope round my body."

"Here it is," replied the witch; "and here is my blue checked apron."

As soon as the rope was tied, the soldier climbed up the tree, and let himself down through the hollow to the ground beneath; and here he found, as the witch had told him, a large hall, in which many hundred lamps were all burning. Then he opened the first door. "Ah!" there sat the dog, with the eyes as large as teacups, staring at him.

"You're a pretty fellow," said the soldier, seizing him, and placing him on the witch's apron, while he filled his pockets from the chest with as many pieces as they would hold. Then he closed the lid, seated the dog upon it again, and walked into another chamber, And, sure enough, there sat the dog with eyes as big as mill-wheels.

"You had better not look at me in that way," said the soldier; "you will make your eyes water;" and then he seated him also upon the apron, and opened the chest. But when he saw what a quantity of silver money it contained, he very quickly threw away all the coppers he had taken, and filled his pockets and his knapsack with nothing but silver.

Then he went into the third room, and there the dog was really hideous; his eyes were, truly, as big as towers, and they turned round and round in his head like wheels.

"Good morning," said the soldier, touching his cap, for he had never seen such a dog in his life. But after looking at him more closely, he thought he had been civil enough, so he placed him on the floor, and opened the chest. Good gracious, what a quantity of gold there was! Enough to buy all the sugar-sticks of the sweet-stuff women; all the tin soldiers, whips, and rocking-horses in the world, or even the whole town itself. There was, indeed, an immense quantity. So the soldier now threw away all the silver money he had taken, and filled his pockets and his knapsack with gold instead; and not only his pockets and his knapsack, but even his cap and boots, so that he could scarcely walk.

He was really rich now; so he replaced the dog on the chest, closed the door, and called up through the tree, "Now pull me out, you old witch."

"Have you got the tinderbox?" asked the witch.

"No; I declare I quite forgot it." So he went back and fetched the tinderbox, and then the witch drew him up out of the tree, and he stood again in the high road, with his pockets, his knapsack, his cap, and his boots full of gold.

"What are you going to do with the tinderbox?" asked the soldier.

"That is nothing to you," replied the witch; "you have the money, now give me the tinderbox."

"I tell you what," said the soldier, "if you don't tell me what you are going to do with it, I will draw my sword and cut off your head."

"No," said the witch.

The soldier immediately cut off her head, and there she lay on the ground. Then he tied up all his money in her apron and slung it on his back like a bundle, put the tinderbox in his pocket, and walked off to the nearest town. It was a very nice town, and he put up at the best inn, and ordered a dinner of all his favorite dishes, for now he was rich and had plenty of money.

The servant, who cleaned his boots, thought they certainly were a shabby pair to be worn by such a rich gentleman, for he had not yet bought any new ones. The next day, however, he procured some good clothes and proper boots, so that our soldier soon became known as a fine gentleman, and the people visited him, and told him all the wonders that were to be seen in the town, and of the king's beautiful daughter, the princess.

"Where can I see her?" asked the soldier.

"She is not to be seen at all," they said; "she lives in a large copper castle, surrounded by walls and towers. No one but the king himself can pass in or out, for there has been a prophecy that she will marry a common soldier, and the king cannot bear to think of such a marriage."

"I should like very much to see her," thought the soldier; but he could not obtain permission to do so. However, he passed a very pleasant time; went to the theatre, drove in the king's garden, and gave a great deal of money to the poor, which was very good of him; he remembered what it had been in olden times to be without a shilling. Now he was rich, had fine clothes, and many friends, who all declared he was a fine fellow and a real gentleman, and all this gratified him exceedingly. But his money would not last forever; and as he spent and gave away a great deal daily, and received none, he found himself at last with only two shillings left. So he was obliged to leave his elegant rooms, and live in a little garret under the roof, where he had to clean his own boots, and even mend them with a large needle. None of his friends came to see him, there were too many stairs to mount up. One dark evening, he had not even a penny to buy a candle; then all at once he remembered that there was a piece of candle stuck in the tinderbox, which he had brought from the old tree, into which the witch had helped him.

He found the tinderbox, but no sooner had he struck a few sparks from the flint and steel, than the door flew open and the dog with eyes as big as teacups, whom he had seen while down in the tree, stood before him, and said, "What orders, master?"

"Hallo," said the soldier; "well this is a pleasant tinderbox, if it brings me all I wish for."

"Bring me some money," said he to the dog.

He was gone in a moment, and presently returned, carrying a large bag of coppers in his mouth. The soldier very soon discovered after this the value of the tinderbox. If he struck the flint once, the dog who sat on the chest of copper money made his appearance; if twice, the dog came from the chest of silver; and if three times, the dog with eyes like towers, who watched over the gold. The soldier had now plenty of money; he returned to his elegant rooms, and reappeared in his fine clothes, so that his friends knew him again directly, and made as much of him as before.

After a while he began to think it was very strange that no one could get a look at the princess. "Everyone says she is very beautiful," thought he to himself; "but what is the use of that if she is to be shut up in a copper castle surrounded by so many towers. Can I buy any means get to see her. Stop! Where is my tinderbox?" Then he struck a light, and in a moment the dog, with eyes as big as teacups, stood before him.

"It is midnight," said the soldier, "yet I should very much like to see the princess, if only for a moment."

The dog disappeared instantly, and before the soldier could even look round, he returned with the princess. She was lying on the dog's back asleep, and looked so lovely, that everyone who saw her would know she was a real princess. The soldier could not help kissing her, true soldier as he was. Then the dog ran back with the princess; but in the morning, while at breakfast with the king and queen, she told them what a singular dream she had had during the night, of a dog and a soldier, that she had ridden on the dog's back, and been kissed by the soldier.

"That is a very pretty story, indeed," said the queen. So the next night one of the old ladies of the court was set to watch by the princess's bed, to discover whether it really was a dream, or what else it might be.

The soldier longed very much to see the princess once more, so he sent for the dog again in the night to fetch her, and to run with her as fast as ever he could. But the old lady put on water boots, and ran after him as quickly as he did, and found that he carried the princess into a large house. She thought it would help her to remember the place if she made a large cross on the door with a piece of chalk. Then she went home to bed, and the dog presently returned with the princess. But when he saw that a cross had been made on the door of the house, where the soldier lived, he took another piece of chalk and made crosses on all the doors in the town, so that the lady-in-waiting might not be able to find out the right door.

Early the next morning the king and queen accompanied the lady and all the officers of the household, to see where the princess had been.

"Here it is," said the king, when they came to the first door with a cross on it.

"No, my dear husband, it must be that one," said the queen, pointing to a second door having a cross also.

"And here is one, and there is another!" they all exclaimed; for there were crosses on all the doors in every direction.

So they felt it would be useless to search any farther. But the queen was a very clever woman; she could do a great deal more than merely ride in a carriage. She took her large gold scissors, cut a piece of silk into squares, and made a neat little bag. This bag she filled with buckwheat flour, and tied it round the princess's neck; and then she cut a small hole in the bag, so that the flour might be scattered on the ground as the princess went along. During the night, the dog came again and carried the princess on his back, and ran with her to the soldier, who loved her very much, and wished that he had been a prince, so that he might have her for a wife. The dog did not observe how the flour ran out of the bag all the way from the castle wall to the soldier's house, and even up to the window, where he had climbed with the princess. Therefore in the morning the king and queen found out where their daughter had been, and the soldier was taken up and put in prison. Oh, how dark and disagreeable it was as he sat there, and the people said to him, "Tomorrow you will be hanged." It was not very pleasant news, and besides, he had left the tinderbox at the inn. In the morning he could see through the iron grating of the little window how the people were hastening out of the town to see him hanged; he heard the drums beating, and saw the soldiers marching. Everyone ran out to look at them and a shoemaker's boy, with a leather apron and slippers on, galloped by so fast, that one of his slippers flew off and struck against the wall where the soldier sat looking through the iron grating. "Hallo, you shoemaker's boy, you need not be in such a hurry," cried the soldier to him. "There will be nothing to see till I come; but if you will run to the house where I have been living, and bring me my tinderbox, you shall have four shillings, but you must put your best foot foremost."

The shoemaker's boy liked the idea of getting the four shillings, so he ran very fast and fetched the tinderbox, and gave it to the soldier. And now we shall see what happened. Outside the town a large gibbet had been erected, round which stood the soldiers and several thousands of people. The king and the queen sat on splendid thrones opposite to the judges and the whole council. The soldier already stood on the ladder; but as they were about to place the rope around his neck, he said that an innocent request was often granted to a poor criminal before he suffered death. He wished very much to smoke a pipe, as it would be the last pipe he should ever smoke in the world. The king could not refuse this request, so the soldier took his tinderbox, and struck fire, once, twice, thrice,— and there in a moment stood all the dogs;—the one with eyes as big as teacups, the one with eyes as large as mill-wheels, and the third, whose eyes were like towers. "Help me now, that I may not be hanged," cried the soldier.

And the dogs fell upon the judges and all the counselors; seized one by the legs, and another by the nose, and tossed them many feet high in the air, so that they fell down and were dashed to pieces.

"I will not be touched," said the king. But the largest dog seized him, as well as the queen, and threw them after the others. Then the soldiers and all the people were afraid, and cried, "Good soldier, you shall be our king, and you shall marry the beautiful princess."

So they placed the soldier in the king's carriage, and the three dogs ran on in front and cried "Hurrah!" and the little boys whistled through their fingers, and the soldiers presented arms. The princess came out of the copper castle, and became queen, which was very pleasing to her. The wedding festivities lasted a whole week, and the dogs sat at the table, and stared with all their eyes.

Some days you're the dog; some days you're the hydrant.
--- Unknown

My essay argues that great art condenses life, eliminating the dull and inappropriate moments. No author demonstrates this better than P.G. Wodehouse (pronounced "Woodhouse" as most of you probably know). To achieve the high comedy beautifully apparent in the following short story, Wodehouse banishes any serious consequences inherent within all the near catastrophes which keep piling up upon poor Bertie Wooster.

From childhood on, I have had a fascination with Ancient Rome. When other boys were playing with toy American soldiers, I had scores of tiny Roman legionnaires. G.I. Joe I found boring; G.I. Julius enthralled me. And I still remember my childhood glee at decoding the I, V, X, L, M, and D's on the cornerstones of downtown buildings which revealed their birth date in Roman numerals. As a youngster I loved everything Latin – especially pig (or "ig-pay-atin-lay" as linguists pronounced it).

Such enthusiasm prompted me to take four years of Latin in high school and then minor in it as an undergraduate. But even with such long-term devotion, I base this column on a respectful disagreement with the Roman author Seneca's most famous literary dictum: "Vita brevis ets, ars longa" – "Life is short, but art is long." The meaning is quite obvious. Our individual lives are brief, but great art (which captures life) is immortal since it is alive for all time. I agree fully with that thought, but it strikes me that the antithesis or opposite statement – "Life is long, but art is short" – more accurately reveals the novel's unique artistic allure.

How can one label our fragile and fleeting time on earth as long? Granted, our time here does seem all too short in general, but it can certainly be all too long in specifics. Weeks, months, years, and even decades have an insidious way of flying by as we age, but that fact does not mitigate the dull truth that a single day, hours, or unfortunate minute can often seem endless. Who among us, during an especially boring lecture, dreadful headache, or lonely weekend has not looked at the clock and then glanced again in hopes it would be an hour later only to discover that not even ten minutes had crept by? And each and every one of our days, though bracing and exciting at times, is stagnated with dull routines: showering and dressing in the morning, driving all over town in the afternoon, worrying ourselves sleepless many nights. These dull and unpleasant minutes add up to hours of our lives each month. Yet we don't begrudge nor resent this waste of time because as adults we recognize it as the foundation of daily life, the routines we endure which somehow make brief encounters with sudden joy, excitement, and inspiration seem all the more rewarding by contrast.

But isn't one of the novel's glories the fact that authors have the godly ability to eliminate all such tedium from their characters' lives? It has been pointed out that in not one of the 40,000 novels written during the Victorian period (1837-1901) did a character ever excuse himself to go to the bathroom. It wasn't prudishness that caused Charles Dickens to eliminate this realistic routine from his books; it was his good sense as an artist. It's bad enough we can't escape this unpleasant chore in our daily lives. We should at least be spared it in our fiction.

Thus, the very treadmills that make life seem tediously long make life in novels seem refreshingly short. Great authors – like all great artists – select only those elements of life best suited to their thematic purposes. Their stories may seem realistic, but they actually have been pruned of all the boredom inherent in our quotidian schedules. Dull days and worthless weeks in a character's life conveniently take place between the end of chapter five and the beginning of chapter six or on occasion, before the first word of chapter one.

What a heaven this earth would be if we were able to write our lives in such a fashion. We would of course edit our paying income taxes. If the I.R.S. agents insisted on an explanation we would inform them that taxes have no thematic purpose in our current life's story, but we would promise that, should we return from the dead for a second edition, then payment and interest will be included in our sequel. Now there's a modern fairy tale that even Seneca and the Ancient Romans would find most appealing.

Episode of the Dog McIntosh

By P.G. Wodehouse

I was jerked from the dreamless by a sound like the rolling of distant thunder; and, the mists of sleep clearing away, was enabled to diagnose this and trace it to its source. It was my Aunt Agatha's dog, McIntosh, scratching at the door. The above, an Aberdeen terrier of weak intellect, had been left in my charge by the old relative while she went off to Aix-les-Bains to take the cure, and I had never been able to make it see eye to eye with me on the subject of early rising. Although a glance at my watch informed me that is was barely ten, here was the animal absolutely up and about.

I pressed the bell, and presently in shimmered Jeeves, complete with tea-tray and preceded by dog, which leaped upon the bed, licked me smartly in the right eye, and immediately curled up and fell into a deep slumber. And where the sense is in getting up at some ungodly hour of the morning and coming scratching at people's doors, when you intend at the first opportunity to go to sleep again, beats me. Nevertheless, every day for the last five weeks this loony hound had pursued the same policy, and I confess I was getting a bit fed.

There were one or two letters on the tray; and, having slipped a refreshing half-cupful into the abyss, I felt equal to dealing with them. The one on top was from my Aunt Agatha.

"Ha!" I said.

"Sir?"

"I said 'Ha!' Jeeves. And I meant 'Ha!' I was registering relief. My Aunt Agatha returns this evening. She will be at her town residence between the hours of six and seven, and she expects to find McIntosh waiting for her on the mat."

"Indeed, sir? I shall miss the little fellow."

"I, too, Jeeves. Despite his habit of rising with the milk and being hearty before breakfast, there is sterling stuff in McIntosh. Nevertheless, I cannot but feel relieved at the prospect of shooting him back to the old home. It has been a guardianship fraught with anxiety. You know what my Aunt Agatha is. She lavishes on that dog a love which might be better be bestowed on a nephew: and if the slightest thing had gone wrong with him while I was *in loco parentis*; if, while in my charge, he had developed rabies or staggers or the botts, I should have been blamed."

"Very true, sir."

"And, as you are aware, London is not big enough to hold Aunt Agatha and anybody she happens to be blaming."

I had opened the second letter, and was giving it the eye.

"Ha!" I said.

"Sir?"

"Once again, 'Ha!' Jeeves, but this time signifying mild surprise. This letter is from Miss Wickham."

"Indeed, sir?"

"And two friends of hers."

"Indeed, sir?"

I sensed – if that is the word I want – the note of concern in the man's voice, and I knew he was saying to himself 'Is the young master about to slip?' You see, there was a time when the Wooster heart was to some extent what you might call ensnared by this Roberta Wickham, and Jeeves had never approved of her. He considered her volatile and frivolous and more or less of a menace to man and beast. And events, I'm bound to day, had rather borne out his view.

"She wants me to give her lunch today."

"Indeed, sir?"

"And two friends of hers."

"Indeed, sir?"

"Here. At one-thirty,"

"Indeed, sir?"

I was piqued.

"Correct this parrot-complex, Jeeves," I said, waving a slice of bread-and-butter rather sternly at the man. "There is no need for you to stand there saying 'Indeed, sir?' I know what you're thinking, and you're wrong. As far as Miss Wickham is concerned, Bertram Wooster is chilled steel. I see no earthly reason why I should not comply with this request. A Wooster may have ceased to love, but he can still be civil."

"Very good, sir."

"Employ the rest of the morning, then, in buzzing to and from and collecting provender. Oh, and roly-poly pudding, Jeeves, with lots of jam in it. Miss Wickham specifically mentions this. Mysterious, what?"

"Extremely, sir."

"Also oysters, ice-cream, and plenty of chocolates with the gooey, slithery stuff in the middle. Makes you sick to think of it, eh?"

"Yes, sir."

"Me, too. But that's what she says. I think she must be on some kind of diet. See to it, Jeeves, will you?"

"Yes, sir."

At half-past twelve I took the dog McIntosh for his morning saunter in the Park; and, returning at about one-ten, found young Bobbie Wickham in the sitting room chatting to Jeeves, who seemed a bit distant, I thought.

I have an idea I've told you about this Bobbie Wickham. Her mother is Lady Wickham, who writes novels which command a ready sale among those who like their literature pretty sloppy. A formidable old bird, rather like my Aunt Agatha in appearance. Bobbie greeted me cordially as I entered – in fact, so cordially that I saw Jeeves pause at the door before biffing off to mix the cocktails and shoot me the sort of grave, warning look a wise old father might pass out to the effervescent son on seeing him going fairly strong with the local vamp. I nodded back, as much as to say 'Chilled steel!' and he oozed out, leaving me to play the sparkling host.

"It was awfully sporting of you to give us this lunch, Bertie," said Bobbie.

"Don't mention it, my dear old thing," I said. "Always a pleasure."

"You got all the stuff I told you about?"

"The garbage, as specified, is in the kitchen. But since when have you become a roly-poly pudding addict?"

"That isn't for me. There's a small boy coming."

"What!"

"I'm awfully sorry," she said. "I know just how you feel and I'm not going to pretend this child isn't pretty near the edge. In fact, he has to be seen to be believed. But it's simply

107

vital that he be cosseted and sucked up to and generally treated as the guest of honour, because everything depends on him."

"How do you mean?"

"I'll tell you. You know mother?"

"Whose mother?"

"My mother."

"Oh, yes. I thought you meant the kid's mother."

"He hasn't got a mother. Only a father, who is a big theatrical manager in America. I met him at a party the other night. Well, mother – my mother – has dramatized one of her novels, and when I met this theatrical manager father, and, between ourselves, made rather a hit with him, I said to myself, why not plant mother's play on him. You see, Bertie, what with one thing and another, my stock isn't very high with mother just now. There was that matter of my smashing up the car. So I thought, here is where I get a chance to put myself right."

"Blumenfield has come to London to see if there's anything in the play line worth buying. So I cooed to him a goodish bit and then asked him if he would listen to mother's play. He said he would, so I asked him to come to lunch and I'd read it to him."

"You're going to read your mother's play – here?" I said, paling.

"I admit it's pretty sticky stuff. But I have an idea that I shall put it over. It all depends on how the kid likes it. You see, old Blumenfield, for some reason, always banks on his verdict. I suppose he thinks the child's intelligence is exactly the same as an average audience's and –"

I uttered a slight yelp, causing Jeeves, who had entered with cocktails, to look at me in a pained sort of way. I had remembered.

"Jeeves!"

"Sir?"

"Do you recollect, when we were in New York, a dish-faced kid of the name of Blumenfield who on a memorable occasion snottered Cyril Bassington-Bassington when the latter tried to go on the stage?"

"Very vividly, sir."

"Well, prepare yourself for a shock. He's coming to lunch."

"Indeed, sir?"

"I don't mind telling you that the prospect of hob-nobbing with him makes me tremble like a leaf. He told Cyril Bassington-Bassington that he had a face like a fish. I give you fair warning that, if he tells me I have a face like a fish, I shall clump his head."

"Bertie!" cried the Wickham.

"Then you'll simply ruin the whole thing."

"I don't care. We Woosters have our pride."

"Perhaps the young gentleman will not notice that you have a face like a fish, sir," suggested Jeeves.

"But we can't just trust to luck," said Bobbie. "It's probably the first thing he will notice."

"In that case, miss," said Jeeves, "it might be the best plan if Mr. Wooster did not attend the luncheon."

I beamed on the man. As always, he had found the way.

"But Mr. Blumenfield will think it odd."

"Well, tell him I'm eccentric. Tell him I have these moods, which come upon me quite suddenly, when I can't stand the sight of people."

"He'll be offended."

"Not half so offended as if I socked his son on the upper maxillary bone."

"I really think it would be the best plan, miss."

"Oh, all right," said Bobbie. "Push off, then. But I wanted you to be here to listen to the play and laugh in the proper places."

"I don't suppose there are any proper places," I said. And with these words I reached the hall in two bounds, grabbed a hat, and made for the street. A cab was just pulling up at the door as I reached it, and inside it were Pop Blumenfield and his foul son. With a slight sinking of the old heart, I saw that the kid had recognized me.

"Hullo!" he said

"Hullo!" I said.

"Where are you off to?" said the kid.

"Ha, ha!" I said, and legged it for the great open spaces.

I lunched at the Drones, doing myself fairly well and lingering pretty considerably over the coffee and cigarettes. At four o'clock I thought it would be safe to think about getting back; but, not wishing to take any chances, I went to the 'phone and rang up the flat.

"All clear, Jeeves?"

"Yes, sir."

"Blumenfield junior nowhere about?"

"No, sir."

"How did everything go off?"

"Quite satisfactorily, I fancy, sir."

"Was I missed?"

"I think Mr. Blumenfield and young Master Blemenfield were somewhat surprised as your absence, sir. Apparently they encountered you as you were leaving the building."

"They did. An awkward moment, Jeeves. Did they comment on this at all?"

"Yes, sir. Indeed, young Master Blumenfield was somewhat outspoken."

"What did he say?"

"I cannot recall his exact words, sir, but he drew a comparison between your mentality and that of a cuckoo."

"A cuckoo, eh?"

"Yes, sir. To the bird's advantage."

"Now you see how right I was to come away. Just one crack like that out of him face to face, and I should infallibly have done his upper maxillary a bit of no good. It was wise of you to suggest that I should lunch out. Well, the coast being clear, I will now return home."

"Before you start, sir, perhaps you would ring Miss Wickham up. She instructed me to desire you to do so. Sloane 8090, Easton Square."

I got the number. And presently young Bobbie's voice came floating over the wire. From the *timbre* I gathered that she was extremely bucked.

"Hullo? Is that you, Bertie?"

"In person. What's the news?"

"Everything went off splendidly. The lunch was just right. The child stuffed himself to the eyebrows and got more and more amiable, till by the time he had had his third go of ice-cream, he was ready to say that any play – even one of mother's – was the goods. I fired it at him before he could come out from under the influence, and he sat there absorbing it in a sort of gorged way, and at the end old Blumenfield said 'Well, sonny, how about it?' and the child gave a sort of faint smile, as if he was thinking about roly-poly pudding, and said 'O.K., pop,' and that's all there was to it. Old Blumenfield has taken him off to the movies, and I'm to look in at the Savoy at five-thirty to sign the contract."

"Terrific!"

"I knew you'd be pleased. Oh, Bertie, there's just one other thing. You remember saying to me once that there wasn't anything in the world you wouldn't do for me?"

I paused a trifle warily. It is true that I had expressed myself in some such terms as she had indicated, but you know how it is. Love's flame flickers and dies, Reason returns to her throne, and you aren't nearly as ready to hop about and jump through hoops as in the first pristine glow of the divine passion.

"What do you want me to do?"

"Well, it's nothing I actually want you to do. It's something I've done that I hope you won't be sticky about. Just before I began reading the play, that dog of yours, the Aberdeen terrier, came into the room. The child Blumenfield was very much taken with it and said he wished he had a dog like that, looking at me in a meaning sort of way. So naturally, I had to say, 'Oh, I'll give you this one!'"

"You...You...What was that?"

"I gave him the dog. I knew you wouldn't mind. You see, it was vital to keep cosseting him. If I'd refused, he would have cut up rough and all that roly-poly pudding and stuff would have been thrown away. You see – "

I hung up. The jaw had fallen, the eyes were protruding. I got to the flat and yelled for Jeeves.

"Jeeves!"

"Sir?"

"The dog...my Aunt Agatha's dog...McIntosh..."

"I have not seen him for some little while, sir. He left me after the conclusion of the luncheon. Possibly he is in your bedroom."

"Yes, and possibly he jolly dashed well isn't. If you want to know where he is, he's in a suite at the Savoy. Miss Wickham has just told me she gave him to Blumenfield junior."

"What was her motive in doing that, sir?"

I explained the circs. Jeeves did a bit of respectful tongue-clicking.

"What are we going to do? Aunt Agatha is due back between the hours of six and seven. She will find herself short one Aberdeen terrier. And, as she will probably have been considerably sea-sick all the way over, you will readily perceive, Jeeves, that, when I break the news that her dog has been given away to a total stranger, I shall find her in no mood of gentle charity."

"I see, sir. Most disturbing. Most disturbing, indeed."

I snorted a trifle.

"Oh?" I said. "And I suppose, if you had been in San Francisco when the earthquake started, you would just have lifted up your finger and said 'Tweet, tweet! Shush, shush! Now, now! Come, come!' The English language, they used to tell me at school, is the richest in the world, crammed full from end to end with about a million red-hot adjectives. Yet the only one you can find to describe this ghastly business is the adjective 'disturbing'. It is not disturbing, Jeeves. It is ... what's the word I want?"

"Cataclysmal, sir?"

"I shouldn't wonder. Well, what's to be done?"

"I will bring you a whiskey-and-soda, sir."

"What's the good of that?"

"It will refresh you, sir. And in the meantime, if it is your wish, I will give the matter consideration. I assume that it is not your desire to do anything that may in any way jeopardize the cordial relations which now exist between Miss Wickham and Mr. and Master Blumenfield" You would not, for example, contemplate proceeding to the Savoy Hotel and demanding the return of the dog?"

It was a tempting thought, but there are things which a Wooster can do and things which a Wooster cannot do. The procedure which he had indicated would undoubtedly have brought home the bacon, but the thwarted kid would have been bound to turn nasty and change his mind about the play. And, while I didn't think that any drama written by Bobbie's mother was likely to do the theatre-going public much good, I couldn't dash the cup of happiness from the blighted girl's lips.

"No, Jeeves," I said. "But if you can think of some way by which I can oil privily into the suite and sneak the animal out of it without causing any hard feelings, spill it."

"I will endeavour to do so, sir."

It was about ten minutes later that he entered the presence once more.

"Yes, Jeeves?"

"I rather fancy, sir, that I have discovered a plan of action which will meet the situation. If I understood you rightly, sir, Mr. and Master Blumenfield have attended a motion-picture performance?"

"Correct."

"In which case, they should not return to the hotel before five-fifteen?"

"Correct once more. Miss Wickham is scheduled to blow in at five-thirty to sign the contract."

"The suite, therefore, is at present unoccupied."

"Except for McIntosh."

"Everything, accordingly, must depend on whether Mr. Blumenfield left instructions that, in the event of her arriving before he did, Miss Wickham was to be shown straight up to the suite, to await his return."

"Why does everything depend on that?"

"Should he have done so, the matter becomes quite simple. All that is necessary is that Miss Wickham shall present herself at the hotel at five o'clock. She will go to the suite. You will also have arrived at the hotel at five, sir, and will have made your way to the corridor outside the suite. If Mr. and Master Blumenfield have not returned, Miss Wickham will open the door and come out and you will go in, secure the dog, and take your departure."

"But I say! Suppose the dog won't come away with me? You know how meager his intelligence is. By this time, especially when he's got used to a new place, he may have forgotten me completely and will look on me as a perfect stranger."

"I had thought of that, sir. The most judicious move will be for you to sprinkle your trousers with aniseed."

"Aniseed?"

"Yes, sir. It is extensively used in the dog-stealing industry."

"But where do you get the stuff?"

"At any chemist's, sir. If you will go out now and procure a small bottle, I will be telephoning to Miss Wickham to apprise her of the contemplated arrangements and ascertain whether she is to be admitted to the suite."

I don't know what the record is for popping out and buying aniseed, but I should think I hold it. The thought of Aunt Agatha getting nearer and nearer to the Metropolis every minute induced a rare burst of speed. I was back at the flat so quick that I nearly met myself coming out.

Jeeves had good news.

"Everything is perfectly satisfactory, sir. Mr. Blumenfield did leave instructions that Miss Wickham was to be admitted to his suite. The young lady is now on her way to the hotel. By the time you reach it, you will find her there."

You know, whatever you say against old Jeeves – and I, for one, have never wavered in my opinion that his views on shirts for evening wear are hidebound and reactionary to a degree – you've got to admit that the man can plan a campaign. Napoleon could have taken his correspondence course.

On the present occasion everything went absolutely according to plan. I had never realized before that dog-stealing could be so simple, having regarded it rather as something that called for the ice-cool brain and the nerve of iron. I see now that a child can do it, if directed by Jeeves. I got to the hotel, sneaked up the stairs, hung about in the corridor trying to look like a potted palm in case anybody came along, and presently the door of the suite opened and Bobbie appeared, and suddenly, as I approached, out shot McIntosh, sniffing passionately, and the next moment his nose was up against my trouserings and he was drinking me in with every evidence of enjoyment. Aniseed isn't a scent that I care for particularly myself, but it seemed to speak straight to the deeps in McIntosh's soul.

The rest was simple. I merely withdrew, followed by the animal. We passed down the stairs in good shape, self reeking to heaven and animal inhaling the bouquet, and after a few anxious moments were safe in a cab, homeward bound.

Arrived at the flat, I handed McIntosh to Jeeves and instructed him to shut him up in the bathroom or somewhere

where the spell cast by my trousers would cease to operate. This done, I again paid the man a marked tribute.

"Jeeves," I said, "I have had occasion to express the view before, and I now express it again fearlessly – you stand in a class of your own."

"Thank you very much, sir. I am glad that everything proceeded satisfactorily."

"The festivities went like a breeze from start to finish. Oh, great Scott!"

"Sir?"

"You've overlooked something, Jeeves."

"Surely not, sir?"

"Yes, Jeeves, I regret to say that the late scheme or plan of action, while gilt-edged as far as I am concerned, has rather landed Miss Wickham in the cart."

"In what way, sir?"

"Why, don't you see that, if they know that she was in the suite at the time of the outrage, the Blumenfields, father and son, will instantly assume that she was mixed up in McIntosh's disappearance, with the result that in their pique and chagrin they will call off the deal about the play.

At this moment there was a ring at the front door bell. And not an ordinary ring, mind you, but one of those resounding peals that suggest that somebody with a high blood-pressure and a grievance stands without.

"Somebody at the door, sir."

"Yes."

"Probably Mr. Blumenfield, senior, sir."

"What!"

"He rang up on the telephone, sir, shortly before you returned, to say that he was about to pay you a call."

"Advise me, Jeeves."

"I fancy the most judicious procedure would be for you to conceal yourself behind the settee, sir."

I saw that his advice was good. I had never met this Bluemenfield socially, but I had seen him from afar, and he hadn't struck me then as a bloke with whom, if in one of his emotional moods, it would be at all agreeable to be shut up in a small room. A large, round, flat, overflowing bird, who might quite easily, if stirred, fall on a fellow and flatten him to the carpet.

So I nestled behind the settee, and in about five seconds there was a sound like a mighty, rushing wind and something extraordinarily substantial bounded into the sitting-room.

"This guy Wooster," bellowed a voice that had been strengthened by a lifetime of ticking actors off at dress-rehearsals from the back of the theatre. "Where is he?"

"I could not say, sir."

"He's sneaked my son's dog."

"Indeed, sir?"

"Walked into my suite as cool as dammit and took the animal away."

"Most disturbing, sir."

"And you don't know where he is?"

"Mr. Wooster may be anywhere, sir. He is uncertain in his movements."

The bloke Blumenfield gave a loud sniff.

"Odd smell here!"

"Yes, sir?"

"What is it?"

"Aniseed, sir."

"Aniseed?"

"Yes, sir. Mr. Wooster sprinkles it on his trousers."

"Sprinkles it on his trousers? What on earth does he do that for?"

"I could not say, sir. Mr. Wooster's motives are always somewhat hard to follow. He is eccentric."

"Eccentric? He must be a loony."

"Yes, sir."

"You mean he is?"

"Yes, sir!"

There was a pause. A long one.

"Oh?" said old Blumenfield, and it seemed to me that a good deal of what you might call the vim had gone out of his voice. He paused again.

"Not *dangerous*?"

"Yes, sir, when roused."

"Er – what rouses him chiefly?"

"One of Mr. Wooster's peculiarities is that he does not like the sight of gentlemen of full habit, sir. They seem to infuriate him."

"You mean, fat men?"

"Yes, sir."

There was another pause. "*I'm* fat!" said old Blumenfield in a rather pensive sort of voice.

"I would not have ventured to suggest it myself, sir, but as you say so ... You may recollect that, on being informed that you were to be a member of the luncheon party, Mr. Wooster, doubting his power of self-control, refused to be present."

"That's right. He went rushing out just as I arrived. I thought it odd at the time. My son thought it odd. We both thought it odd."

"Yes, sir. Mr. Wooster, I imagine, wished to avoid any possible unpleasantness, such as has occurred before ... With regard to the smell of aniseed, sir, I fancy I have now located it. Unless I am mistaken it proceeds from behind the settee. No doubt Mr. Wooster is sleeping there.

"Does he often sleep on the floor?"

"Most afternoons, sir. Would you desire me to wake him?"

"No!"

"I thought you had something that you wished to say to Mr. Wooster, sir."

Old Blumenfield drew a deep breath. "So did I," he said. "But I find I haven't. Just get me alive out of here, that's all I ask."

I heard the door close, and a little while later the front door banged. I crawled out. Jeeves came trickling back.

"Gone, Jeeves?"

"Yes, sir."

I bestowed an approving look on him.

"One of your best efforts, Jeeves."

"Thank you, sir."

"But what beats me is why he ever came here. What made him think that I had sneaked McIntosh away?"

"I took the liberty of recommending Miss Wickham to tell Mr. Blumenfield that she had observed you removing the animal from his suite, sir. The point which you raised regarding the possibility of her being suspected of complicity in the affair had not escaped me. It seemed to me that this would establish her solidly in Mr. Blumenfield's good opinion."

"I see. Risky, of course, but possibly justified. Yes, on the whole, justified. What's that you've got there?"

"A five pound note, sir. One Mr. Blumenfield gave me."

"Eh? Why did he give you a fiver?"

"He very kindly presented it to me on my handing him the dog, sir."

I gaped at the man.

"You don't mean to say -- ?"

"Not McIntosh, sir. McIntosh is at present in my bedroom. This was another animal of the same species which I purchased at the shop in Bond Street during your absence. Except to the eye of love, one Aberdeen terrier looks very much like another Aberdeen terrier, sir. Mr. Blumenfield, I am happy to say, did not detect the innocent subterfuge."

"Jeeves," I said – and I am not ashamed to confess that there was a spot of chokiness in the voice – "there is none like you, none."

"Thank you very much, sir."

"Owing solely to the fact that your head bulges in unexpected spots, thus enabling you to do about twice as much bright thinking in any given time as any other two men in existence, happiness, you might say, reigns supreme. Aunt Agatha is on velvet, I am on velvet, the Wickhams, mother and daughter, are on velvet, the Blumenfields, father and son, are on velvet. As far as the eye can reach, a solid mass of humanity, owing to you, all on velvet. A fiver is not sufficient, Jeeves. If I thought the world thought that Bertram Wooster thought a measly five pounds an adequate reward for such services as yours, I should never hold my head up again. Have another?"

"Thank you sir."

"And one more?"

"Thank you very much, sir."

"And a third for luck?"

"Really sir, I am exceedingly obliged. Excuse me sir, I fancy I heard the telephone."

He pushed out into the hall, and I heard him doing a good deal of the "Yes, madam, " "Certainly, madam!" stuff. Then he came back.

"Mrs. Spenser Gregson on the telephone, sir."

"Aunt Agatha?"

"Yes, sir. Speaking from Victoria Station. She desires to communicate with you with reference to the dog McIntosh. I gather that she wishes to hear from your own lips that all is well with the little fellow, sir."

I straightened the tie. I pulled down the waistcoat. I snapped the cuffs. I felt absolutely all-righto.

"Lead me to her," I said.

You think dogs will not be in heaven? I tell you, they will be there long before any of us. --- Robert Louis Stevenson

I don't think a teenager could quite understand Saki's ironic connection between Attab and the sparrow with Jocantha and Bertie in "The Philanthropist and the Happy Cat" nor perhaps comprehend the depth of Kipling's torn heart in "The Power of the Dog." As my essay speculates, this is why we have no fifteen-year-old English majors at our universities.

You probably notice that we have placed a cat story in among these dog tales. But if you have to ask yourself why we did this, then you certainly do not understand cats. For if there is one thing that applies to most felines, it is that they love to wander off to places they should not be, and they love to make sure that dogs are not getting all the attention!

During the many years that I have been on a leave of absence from my university, I've been in the peculiar position of a teacher who has lectured to tens of thousands of students, not one of whom he can claim as his own. I have lost count of the number of literary assemblies I've given at elementary, middle, and high schools throughout the country; yet when I finish my lecture the students return to someone else's class.

I really miss having my own students. Although I would like to believe that my assembly appearances might encourage or even inspire a few students to read a particular author, that accomplishment hardly compares to the deepening relationship a classroom teacher enjoys – I use that verb loosely – with students through discussions, conferences, thought journals, and paper-grading.

Perhaps I miss the classroom most on the night before a fall or spring semester begins. When I taught at UCLA, the class rosters were always put in our faculty boxes the weekend before the Monday when classes began. I would drive over to the English office on Sunday evening to collect my class rosters and gaze at the alphabetized names. Usually they were all unknown except for an occasional student who was taking a second class from me. Next to his or her name I would jot down GFP ("Glutton for Punishment").

Obviously a name on a roster reveals little. I did once have a student named Herman Sturmann. I assumed he would have had a Dickensian childhood since his parents demonstrated their sadistic streak upon naming him. Before I called the roll on the first day he informed me that he preferred being called "Chad," his middle name. Indeed, who wouldn't under those circumstances??

I remember one Sunday evening before classes began when I received a phone call from a friend who taught in the physics department. He too had retrieved his class roster early and he excitedly told me that the name "Lee Chan" appeared on it. The name was familiar to me because Mr. Chan was all of fourteen years old. He was one of those prodigies who had scored 750 on his Math SAT exam when he was twelve and had therefore been on his way to college before I had been on my way to Bar Mitzvah.

It struck me that night that all of the prodigies I had ever heard of entering college at an astonishingly early age, not one of them had ever majored in English. All seemed headed for a concentration in science or math. Was this because a genius did not want to squander his or her talent on a field as notoriously paycheck-challenged as English education?

I don't think so. I believe that it has to do with maturity. No matter how intellectually advanced an adolescent might be, he needs a very different type of gift to be an outstanding English major. The finest students of English literature would be those who have *lived*, those who have experienced the joys, sorrows, moral ambiguities and ethical challenges that give depth and meaning to our individual lives.

I have always been proud of the fact that to be a brilliant student in my academic subject, it might help to be intellectual, but it is imperative to possess both sensitivity and empathy, two qualities not even a fourteen-year-old Einstein could fully possess. That is why English professors tend to value adult students. What age might occasionally diminish in intellectual quickness or abstract reasoning, it more than compensates for in emotional maturity and literary insights. I do miss teaching my eighteen-year-old students, but it is the forty-eight and sixty-eight- year- olds whom I often remember most fondly. It is they who frequently turn the lectern around and teach me so much.

The Philanthropist and The Happy Cat

By Saki

JOCANTHA BESSBURY was in the mood to be serenely and graciously happy. Her world was a pleasant place, and it was wearing one of its pleasantest aspects. Gregory had managed to get home for a hurried lunch and a smoke afterwards in the little snuggery; the lunch had been a good one, and there was just time to do justice to the coffee and cigarettes. Both were excellent in their way, and Gregory was, in his way, an excellent husband. Jocantha rather suspected herself of making him a very charming wife, and more than suspected herself of having a first-rate dressmaker.

"I don't suppose a more thoroughly contented personality is to be found in all Chelsea," observed Jocantha in allusion to herself; "except perhaps Attab," she continued, glancing towards the large tabby-marked cat that lay in considerable ease in a corner of the divan. "He lies there, purring and dreaming, shifting his limbs now and then in an ecstasy of cushioned comfort. He seems the incarnation of everything soft and silky and velvety, without a sharp edge in his composition, a dreamer whose philosophy is sleep and let sleep; and then, as evening draws on, he goes out into the garden with a red glint in his eyes and slays a drowsy sparrow."

"As every pair of sparrows hatches out ten or more young ones in the year, while their food supply remains stationary, it is just as well that the Attabs of the community should have that idea of how to pass an amusing afternoon," said Gregory. Having delivered himself of this sage comment he lit another cigarette, bade Jocantha a playfully affectionate good-bye, and departed into the outer world.

"Remember, dinner's a wee bit earlier tonight, as we're going to the Haymarket," she called after him.

Left to herself, Jocantha continued the process of looking at her life with placid, introspective eyes. If she had not everything she wanted in this world, at least she was very well pleased with what she had got. She was very well pleased, for instance, with the snuggery, which contrived somehow to be cozy and dainty and expensive all at once. The porcelain was rare and beautiful, the Chinese enamels took on wonderful tints in the firelight, the rugs and hangings led the eye through sumptuous harmonies of colouring. It was a room in which one might have suitably entertained an ambassador or an archbishop, but it was also a room in which one could cut out pictures for a scrapbook without feeling that one was scandalizing the deities of the place with one's litter. And as with the snuggery, so with the rest of the house, and as with the house, so with the other departments of Jocantha's life; she really had good reason for being one of the most contented women in Chelsea.

From being in a mood of simmering satisfaction with her lot she passed to the phase of being generously commiserating for those thousands around her whose lives and circumstances were dull, cheap, pleasureless, and empty. Work girls, shop assistants and so forth, the class that have neither the happy-go-lucky freedom of the poor nor the leisured freedom of the rich, came specially within the range of her sympathy. It was sad to think that there were young people who, after a long day's work, had to sit alone in chill, dreary bedrooms because they could not afford the price of a cup of coffee and a sandwich in a restaurant, still less a shilling for a theatre gallery.

Jocantha's mind was still dwelling on this theme when she started forth on an afternoon campaign of desultory shopping; it would be rather a comforting thing, she told herself, if she could do something, on the spur of the moment, to bring a gleam of pleasure and interest into the life of even one or two wistful-hearted, empty-pocketed workers; it would add a good deal to her sense of enjoyment at the theatre that night. She would get two upper circle tickets for a popular play, make her way into some cheap tea-shop, and present the tickets to the first couple of interesting work girls with whom she could casually drop into conversation. She could explain matters by saying that she was unable to use the tickets herself and did not want them to be wasted, and, on the other hand, did not want the trouble of sending them back. On further reflection she decided that it might be better to get only one ticket and give it to some lonely-looking girl sitting eating her frugal meal by herself; the girl might scrape acquaintance with her next-seat neighbour at the theatre and lay the foundations of a lasting friendship.

With the Fairy Godmother impulse strong upon her, Jocantha marched into a ticket agency and selected with immense care an upper circle seat for the "Yellow Peacock," a play that was attracting a considerable amount of discussion and criticism. Then she went forth in search of a tea-shop and philanthropic adventure, at about the same time that Attab sauntered into the garden with a mind attuned to sparrow stalking. In a corner of an A.B.C. shop she found an unoccupied table, whereat she promptly installed herself, impelled by the fact that at the next table was sitting a young girl, rather plain of feature, with tired, listless eyes, and a general air of uncomplaining forlornness. Her dress was of poor material, but aimed at being in the fashion, her hair was pretty, and her complexion bad; she was finishing a modest meal of tea and scone, and she was not very different in her way from thousands of other girls who were finishing, or beginning, or continuing their teas in London tea-shops at that exact moment. The odds were enormously in favour of the supposition that she had never seen the "Yellow Peacock"; obviously she supplied excellent material for Jocantha's first experiment in haphazard benefaction.

Jocantha ordered some tea and a muffin, and then turned a friendly scrutiny on her neighbour with a view to catching her eye. At that precise moment the girl's face lit up with sudden pleasure, her eyes sparkled, a flush came into her cheeks, and she looked almost pretty. A young man, whom she greeted with an affectionate "Hullo, Bertie," came up to her table and took his seat in a chair facing her. Jocantha looked hard at the new-comer; he was in appearance a few years younger than herself, very much better looking than Gregory, rather better looking, in fact, than any of the young men of her set. She guessed him to be a well-mannered young clerk in some wholesale warehouse, existing and amusing himself as best he might on a tiny salary, and commanding a holiday of about two weeks in the year. He was aware, of course, of his good looks, but with the shy self-consciousness of the Anglo-Saxon, not the blatant complacency of the Latin or Semite. He was obviously on terms of friendly intimacy with the girl he was talking to, probably they were drifting towards a formal engagement. Jocantha pictured the boy's home, in a rather narrow circle, with a tiresome mother who always wanted to know how and where he spent his evenings. He would exchange that humdrum thraldom in due course for a home of his own, dominated by a chronic scarcity of pounds, shillings, and pence, and a dearth of most of the things that made life attractive or comfortable. Jocantha felt extremely sorry for him. She wondered if he had seen the "Yellow Peacock"; the odds were enormously in favour of the supposition that he had not. The girl had finished her tea and would shortly be going back to her work; when the boy was alone it would be quite easy for Jocantha to say: "My husband has made other arrangements for me this evening; would you care to make use of this ticket, which would otherwise be wasted?" Then she could come there again one afternoon for tea, and, if she saw him, ask him how he liked the play. If he was a nice boy and improved on acquaintance he could be given more theatre tickets, and perhaps asked to come one Sunday to tea at Chelsea. Jocantha made up her mind that he would improve on acquaintance, and that Gregory would like him, and that the Fairy Godmother business would prove far more entertaining than she had originally anticipated. The boy was distinctly presentable; he knew how to brush his hair, which was possibly an imitative faculty; he knew what colour of tie suited him, which might be intuition; he was exactly the type that Jocantha admired, which of course was accident. Altogether she was rather pleased when the girl looked at the clock and bade a friendly but hurried farewell to her companion. Bertie nodded "good-bye," gulped down a mouthful of tea, and then produced from his overcoat pocket a paper-covered book, bearing the title "Sepoy and Sahib, a tale of the great Mutiny."

The laws of tea-shop etiquette forbid that you should offer theatre tickets to a stranger without having first caught the stranger's eye. It is even better if you can ask to have a sugar basin passed to you, having previously concealed the fact that you have a large and well-filled sugar basin on your own table; this is not difficult to manage, as the printed menu is generally nearly as large as the table, and can be made to stand on end.

Jocantha set to work hopefully; she had a long and rather high-pitched discussion with the waitress concerning alleged defects in an altogether blameless muffin, she made loud and plaintive inquiries about the tube service to some impossibly remote suburb, she talked with brilliant insincerity to the tea-shop kitten, and as a last resort she upset a milk-jug and swore at it daintily. Altogether she attracted a good deal of attention, but never for a moment did she attract the attention of the boy with the beautifully-brushed hair, who was some thousands of miles away in the baking plains of Hindostan, amid deserted bungalows, seething bazaars, and riotous barrack squares, listening to the throbbing of tom-toms and the distant rattle of musketry.

Jocantha went back to her house in Chelsea, which struck her for the first time as looking dull and over-furnished. She had a resentful conviction that Gregory would be uninteresting at dinner, and that the play would be stupid after dinner. On the whole her frame of mind showed a marked divergence from the purring complacency of Attab, who was again curled up in his corner of the divan with a great peace radiating from every curve of his body.

But then he had killed his sparrow.

The Power of the Dog

By Rudyard Kipling

There is sorrow enough in the natural way
From men and women to fill our day;
And when we are certain of sorrow in store,
Why do we always arrange for more?
Brothers and Sisters, I bid you beware
Of giving your heart to a dog to tear.

Buy a pup and your money will buy
Love unflinching that cannot lie --
Perfect passion and worship fed
By a kick in the ribs or a pat on the head.
Nevertheless it is hardly fair
To risk your heart for a dog to tear.

When the fourteen years which Nature permits
Are closing in asthma, or tumour, or fits,
And the vet's unspoken prescription runs
To lethal chambers or loaded guns,
Then you will find—it's your own affair --
But . . . you've given your heart to a dog to tear.

When the body that lived at your single will,
With its whimper of welcome, is stilled (how still!)
When the spirit that answered your every mood
Is gone—wherever it goes—for good,
You will discover how much you care,
And will give your heart to a dog to tear.

We've sorrow enough in the natural way,
When it comes to burying Christian clay.
Our loves are not given, but only lent,
At compound interest of cent per cent.
Though it is not always the case, I believe,

That the longer we've kept'em, the more do we grieve;

For, when debts are payable, right or wrong,
A short-time loan is as bad as a long --
So why in Heaven (before we are there)
Should we give our hearts to a dog to tear?

The more one comes to know men, the more one comes to admire the dog.
--- Joussenel

> *The connection between the Johnny Appleseed of my essay and the wizard in L. Frank Baum's story (no, not THAT wizard) is that both are uniquely American stories. The cynicism of the wizard is as American in nature as the selflessness of Appleseed's fruitful mission.*

I want to share with you a famous children's story and its enormous influence on my future career. I admit that as a ten-year-old, my greatest reading enthusiasm was for Superman comic books. I didn't find anything in the stories we read at school that could match the pure excitement nor mythic elements of the caped crusader from the planet Krypton.

But my fifth grade teacher, Miss Walls, introduced me to a much more personal literary myth than Superman and converted me to a lifetime of better reading. Every Friday afternoon during the last hour of the week Miss Walls read aloud to the class. One day she brought in a large volume that she told us had been her great-grandmother's.

From it she read us the strange story of a baby born in Massachusetts in 1774 who gazed out the window after a heavy rain and discovered that a rainbow ended in the boughs of a huge apple tree in his front yard. The tree was in full bloom with white blossoms which the rainbow had turned into every color imaginable.

The baby's name was John Chapman. The Chapman family moved to Pennsylvania a few years later and there, as a boy, John decided on his life's mission. Inspired by that extraordinary tree, he dedicated his life to planting apple orchards thick and strong from Pennsylvania to the rest of the country. Every autumn he would go to the cider presses, collect the mashed pulp, separate the seeds, wash and dry them, and pour them into flour sacks. For the rest of his life he walked across America spreading the seeds from his sacks at river banks, empty meadows, and yards large and small. He eventually walked as far south as Tennessee and as far west as the Rocky Mountains, and by giving seeds to the pioneers his trees eventually reached the West Coast. Thus was born the legend of Johnny Appleseed.

The story was good, but what made it unforgettable was what happened next. When Miss Walls finished the story there were about twenty minutes left before dismissal. She told us to put on our jackets and she led us to the playground. Behind it, separating the school from a housing development was a field filled with apple trees. She explained that because the city we lived in – Indianapolis – was on the Old National Road (US 40 when I was a child; Interstate 70 today) there was every chance that this orchard came from seeds Johnny Appleseed originally planted. The National Road had been his highway west, and he had even died in Indiana. Here was a Superman who had actually stood where I was now standing.

The next morning Miss Walls had placed an apple sliced in two on each desk. We were to count the seeds in our apple; mine had only three. "Do you see," she asked, "how easy it is to count the number of seeds in an apple?" We did.

She then asked us to put one seed in the palm of our hand and examine it. "No matter how closely you look at it," she continued, "you'll never be able to count how many apples are in that seed." We looked puzzled until she explained that every time Johnny Appleseed planted a seed, it became a tree that could produce hundreds and hundreds of apples in its long lifetime.

She then reminded us that we brought apples to our teachers because the apple was the symbol of the teaching profession. "All teachers," she said, "are Johnny Appleseeds and you, students, are my seeds that I plant with knowledge. If I do a good job, that knowledge will later blossom forth from you into your children, and into their children, and into their children, until the end of time."

I was sold. I'm sure I entered the teaching profession still inspired by Johnny Appleseed. I now view each dab of Dickens, bit of Brontë, and dollop of Trollope that I lecture on as so many scholarly seeds that I plant within my students and audiences. And I'm always hopeful that they will take this knowledge, mix it within the rich soil of their own personal experiences, and, ultimately, with luck, disseminate it from here to eternity.

Glass Dog: An American Fairy Tale

By L. Frank Baum

An accomplished wizard once lived on the top floor of a tenement house and passed his time in thoughtful study and studious thought. What he didn't know about wizardry was hardly worth knowing, for he possessed all the books and recipes of all the wizards who had lived before him; and, moreover, he had invented several wizardments himself.

This admirable person would have been completely happy but for the numerous interruptions to his studies caused by folk who came to consult him about their troubles (in which he was not interested), and by the loud knocks of the iceman, the milkman, the baker's boy, the laundryman and the peanut woman. He never dealt with any of these people; but they rapped at his door every day to see him about this or that or to try to sell him their wares. Just when he was most deeply interested in his books or engaged in watching the bubbling of a cauldron there would come a knock at his door. And after sending the intruder away he always found he had lost his train of thought or ruined his compound.

At length these interruptions aroused his anger, and he decided he must have a dog to keep people away from his door. He didn't know where to find a dog, but in the next room lived a poor glass-blower with whom he had a slight acquaintance; so he went into the man's apartment and asked:

"Where can I find a dog?"

"What sort of a dog?" inquired the glass-blower.

"A good dog. One that will bark at people and drive them away. One that will be no trouble to keep and won't expect to be fed. One that has no fleas and is neat in his habits. One that will obey me when I speak to him. In short, a good dog," said the wizard.

"Such a dog is hard to find," returned the glass-blower, who was busy making a blue glass flower pot with a pink glass rosebush in it, having green glass leaves and yellow glass roses.

The wizard watched him thoughtfully.

"Why cannot you blow me a dog out of glass?" he asked, presently.

"I can," declared the glass-blower; "but it would not bark at people, you know."

"Oh, I'll fix that easily enough," replied the other. "If I could not make a glass dog bark I would be a mighty poor wizard."

"Very well; if you can use a glass dog I'll be pleased to blow one for you. Only, you must pay for my work."

"Certainly," agreed the wizard. "But I have none of that horrid stuff you call money. You must take some of my wares in exchange."

The glass-blower considered the matter for a moment.

"Could you give me something to cure my rheumatism?" he asked.

"Oh, yes; easily."

"Then it's a bargain. I'll start the dog at once. What color of glass shall I use?"

"Pink is a pretty color," said the wizard, "and it's unusual for a dog, isn't it?"

"Very," answered the glass-blower; "but it shall be pink."

So the wizard went back to his studies and the glass-blower began to make the dog.

Next morning he entered the wizard's room with the glass dog under his arm and set it carefully upon the table. It was a beautiful pink in color, with a fine coat of spun glass, and about its neck was twisted a blue glass ribbon. Its eyes were specks of black glass and sparkled intelligently, as do many of the glass eyes worn by men.

The wizard expressed himself pleased with the glass-blower's skill and at once handed him a small vial.

"This will cure your rheumatism," he said.

"But the vial is empty!" protested the glass-blower.

"Oh, no; there is one drop of liquid in it," was the wizard's reply.

"Will one drop cure my rheumatism?" inquired the glass-blower, in wonder.

"Most certainly. That is a marvelous remedy. The one drop contained in the vial will cure instantly any kind of disease ever known to humanity. Therefore it is especially good for rheumatism. But guard it well, for it is the only drop of its kind in the world, and I've forgotten the recipe."

"Thank you," said the glass-blower, and went back to his room.

Then the wizard cast a wizzy spell and mumbled several very learned words in the wizardese language over the glass dog. Whereupon the little animal first wagged its tail from side to side, then winked his left eye knowingly, and at last began barking in a most frightful manner—that is, when you stop to consider the noise came from a pink glass dog. There is something almost astonishing in the magic arts of wizards; unless, of course, you know how to do the things yourself, when you are not expected to be surprised at them.

The wizard was as delighted as a school teacher at the success of his spell, although he was not astonished. Immediately he placed the dog outside his door, where it would bark at anyone who dared knock and so disturb the studies of its master.

The glass-blower, on returning to his room, decided not to use the one drop of wizard cure-all just then.

"My rheumatism is better today," he reflected, "and I will be wise to save the medicine for a time when I am very ill, when it will be of more service to me."

So he placed the vial in his cupboard and went to work blowing more roses out of glass. Presently he happened to think the medicine might not keep, so he started to ask the wizard about it. But when he reached the door the glass dog barked so fiercely that he dared not knock, and returned in great haste to his own room. Indeed, the poor man was quite upset at so unfriendly a reception from the dog he had himself so carefully and skillfully made.

The next morning, as he read his newspaper, he noticed an article stating that the beautiful Miss Mydas, the richest young lady in town, was very ill, and the doctors had given up hope of her recovery.

The glass-blower, although miserably poor, hard-working and homely of feature, was a man of ideas. He suddenly recollected his precious medicine, and determined to use it to better advantage than relieving his own ills. He dressed himself in his best clothes, brushed his hair and combed his whiskers, washed his hands and tied his necktie, blackened his hoes and sponged his vest, and then put the vial of magic cure-all in his pocket. Next he locked his door, went downstairs and walked through the streets to the grand mansion where the wealthy Miss Mydas resided.

The butler opened the door and said:

"No soap, no chromos, no vegetables, no hair oil, no books, no baking powder. My young lady is dying and we're well supplied for the funeral."

The glass-blower was grieved at being taken for a peddler.

"My friend," he began, proudly; but the butler interrupted him, saying:

"No tombstones, either; there's a family graveyard and the monument's built."

"The graveyard won't be needed if you will permit me to speak," said the glass-blower.

"No doctors, sir; they've given up my young lady, and she's given up the doctors," continued the butler, calmly.

"I'm no doctor," returned the glass-blower.

"Nor are the others. But what is your errand?"

"I called to cure your young lady by means of a magical compound."

"Step in, please, and take a seat in the hall. I'll speak to the housekeeper," said the butler, more politely.

So he spoke to the housekeeper and the housekeeper mentioned the matter to the steward and the steward consulted the chef and the chef kissed the lady's maid and sent her to see the stranger. Thus are the very wealthy hedged around with ceremony, even when dying.

When the lady's maid heard from the glass-blower that he had a medicine which would cure her mistress, she said:

"I'm glad you came."

"But," said he, "if I restore your mistress to health she must marry me."

"I'll make inquiries and see if she's willing," answered the maid, and went at once to consult Miss Mydas.

The young lady did not hesitate an instant.

"I'd marry any old thing rather than die!" she cried. "Bring him here at once!"

So the glass-blower came, poured the magic drop into a little water, gave it to the patient, and the next minute Miss Mydas was as well as she had ever been in her life.

"Dear me!" she exclaimed; "I've an engagement at the Fritters' reception tonight. Bring my pearl-colored silk, Marie, and I will begin my toilet at once. And don't forget to cancel the order for the funeral flowers and your mourning gown."

"But, Miss Mydas," remonstrated the glass-blower, who stood by, "you promised to marry me if I cured you."

"I know," said the young lady, "but we must have time to make proper announcement in the society papers and have the wedding cards engraved. Call tomorrow and we'll talk it over."

The glass-blower had not impressed her favorably as a husband, and she was glad to find an excuse for getting rid of him for a time. And she did not want to miss the Fritters' reception.

Yet the man went home filled with joy; for he thought his stratagem had succeeded and he was about to marry a rich wife who would keep him in luxury forever afterward.

The first thing he did on reaching his room was to smash his glass-blowing tools and throw them out of the window.

He then sat down to figure out ways of spending his wife's money.

The following day he called upon Miss Mydas, who was reading a novel and eating chocolate creams as happily as if she had never been ill in her life.

"Where did you get the magic compound that cured me?" she asked.

"From a learned wizard," said he; and then, thinking it would interest her, he told how he had made the glass dog for the wizard, and how it barked and kept everybody from bothering him.

"How delightful!" she said. "I've always wanted a glass dog that could bark."

"But there is only one in the world," he answered, "and it belongs to the wizard."

"You must buy it for me," said the lady.

"The wizard cares nothing for money," replied the glass-blower.

"Then you must steal it for me," she retorted. "I can never live happily another day unless I have a glass dog that can bark."

The glass-blower was much distressed at this, but said he would see what he could do. For a man should always try to please his wife, and Miss Mydas has promised to marry him within a week.

On his way home he purchased a heavy sack, and when he passed the wizard's door and the pink glass dog ran out to bark at him he threw the sack over the dog, tied the opening with a piece of twine, and carried him away to his own room.

The next day he sent the sack by a messenger boy to Miss Mydas, with his compliments, and later in the afternoon he called upon her in person, feeling quite sure he would be received with gratitude for stealing the dog she so greatly desired.

But when he came to the door and the butler opened it, what was his amazement to see the glass dog rush out and begin barking at him furiously.

"Call off your dog," he shouted, in terror.

"I can't, sir," answered the butler. "My young lady has ordered the glass dog to bark whenever you call here. You'd better look out, sir," he added, "for if it bites you, you may have glassophobia!"

This so frightened the poor glass-blower that he went away hurriedly. But he stopped at a drug store and put his last dime in the telephone box so he could talk to Miss Mydas without being bitten by the dog.

"Give me Pelf 6742!" he called.

"Hello! What is it?" said a voice.

"I want to speak with Miss Mydas," said the glass-blower.

Presently a sweet voice said: "This is Miss Mydas. What is it?"

"Why have you treated me so cruelly and set the glass dog on me?" asked the poor fellow.

"Well, to tell the truth," said the lady, "I don't like your looks. Your cheeks are pale and baggy, your hair is coarse and long, your eyes are small and red, your hands are big and rough, and you are bow-legged."

"But I can't help my looks!" pleaded the glass-blower; "and you really promised to marry me."

"If you were better looking I'd keep my promise," she returned. "But under the circumstances you are no fit mate for me, and unless you keep away from my mansion I shall set my glass dog on you!" Then she dropped the 'phone and would have nothing more to say.

The miserable glass-blower went home with a heart bursting with disappointment and began tying a rope to the bedpost by which to hang himself.

Someone knocked at the door, and, upon opening it, he saw the wizard.

"I've lost my dog," he announced.

"Have you, indeed?" replied the glass-blower tying a knot in the rope.

"Yes; someone has stolen him."

"That's too bad," declared the glass-blower, indifferently.

"You must make me another," said the wizard.

"But I cannot; I've thrown away my tools."

"Then what shall I do?" asked the wizard.

"I do not know, unless you offer a reward for the dog."

"But I have no money," said the wizard.

"Offer some of your compounds, then," suggested the glass-blower, who was making a noose in the rope for his head to go through.

"The only thing I can spare," replied the wizard, thoughtfully, "is a Beauty Powder."

"What!" cried the glass-blower, throwing down the rope, "have you really such a thing?"

"Yes, indeed. Whoever takes the powder will become the most beautiful person in the world."

"If you will offer that as a reward," said the glass-blower, eagerly, "I'll try to find the dog for you, for above everything else I long to be beautiful."

"But I warn you the beauty will only be skin deep," said the wizard.

"That's all right," replied the happy glass-blower; "when I lose my skin I shan't care to remain beautiful."

"Then tell me where to find my dog and you shall have the powder," promised the wizard.

So the glass-blower went out and pretended to search, and by-and-by he returned and said:

"I've discovered the dog. You will find him in the mansion of Miss Mydas."

The wizard went at once to see if this were true, and, sure enough, the glass dog ran out and began barking at him. Then the wizard spread out his hands and chanted a magic spell which sent the dog fast asleep, when he picked him up and carried him to his own room on the top floor of the tenement house.

Afterward he carried the Beauty Powder to the glass-blower as a reward, and the fellow immediately swallowed it and became the most beautiful man in the world.

The next time he called upon Miss Mydas there was no dog to bark at him, and when the young lady saw him she fell in love with his beauty at once.

"If only you were a count or a prince," she sighed, "I'd willingly marry you."

"But I am a prince," he answered; "the Prince of Dogblowers."

"Ah!" said she; "then if you are willing to accept an allowance of four dollars a week I'll order the wedding cards engraved."

The man hesitated, but when he thought of the rope hanging from his bedpost he consented to the terms.

So they were married, and the bride was very jealous of her husband's beauty and led him a dog's life. So he managed to get into debt and made her miserable in turn.

As for the glass dog, the wizard set him barking again by means of his wizardness and put him outside his door. I suppose he is there yet, and am rather sorry, for I should like to consult the wizard about the moral to this story.

Both Anstey's story and Morley's Commandments emphasize the passionate commitment which dogs must make to their families. My essay on holidays notes that half of our twelve annual holidays are grounded within the same sense of fierce commitment. I realize that the connection between my essay and the two dog stories is very far-fetched, but who better to fetch something so far than dogs?

April was always a special month for Charles Dickens. His first novel, *Pickwick Papers*, not only first appeared on April Fool's Day, but he created Mr. Pickwick and the other Pickwickians to represent the most gullible of April fools. In spirit, April 1st remains a much more British than American holiday.

But if we examine all the holidays we celebrate here in America we learn a great deal about our values as a nation. If we eliminate religious holidays, since they exclude those not of a certain faith, and eliminate the Birthdays (Lincoln, Washington, King), since they celebrate a life rather than an ideal, we are left with twelve secular holidays. Although they seem widely varied, the holidays actually divide evenly into just two rather surprising categories.

Six of the twelve celebrate Commitment and Duty: the demanding role of Soldier (Veteran's and Memorial Days), Worker (Labor Day), Faithful Lover (Valentine's Day), and perhaps the hardest commitments – Mother's and Father's Day. I remember as a youngster asking a teacher why there was no Children's Day. "Because EVERY day is Children's Day," she sighed wearily.

Oddly, the other six holidays celebrate the very opposite ideal from duty – Freedom: Political (July 4th), Religious (Thanksgiving), Alcoholic (St. Patrick's Day!), Freedom from our past mistakes (New Year's Day), Freedom from our fear of future death (Halloween, with all the comic ghosts, cadavers, and skeletons) and Freedom from taste and restraint (April Fool's Day).

The Commitment Holidays are observed quite solemnly with mealtime prayers at Thanksgiving, gravesite ceremonies on Memorial Day, familial visits and sentimental cards to our parents in May and June. The Freedom Holidays, of course, are celebrated wildly with fireworks on the Fourth, trick-or-treating on Halloween, green beer on St. Paddy's Day, noisemakers on New Year's, and practical jokes on April Fool's.

Why would we Americans choose to celebrate such opposing ideals as duty and freedom? I suppose it is because we know that these particular values are at heart quite similar and complementary. On New Year's Eve, for example, we may try to drown out thoughts of duty with champagne and noisemakers, but we also use the very next day to think up the most binding (not to mention unrealistic) resolutions for the coming twelve months. And though Memorial Day honors those who gave the ultimate commitment to our country, the gravesite speeches always focus on one subject more than any other: freedom.

And aren't we Americans clever to parcel out just about one holiday per month to keep our celebrations spread evenly throughout the year: January's New Year; February's Valentine; March's St. Patrick; April Fool's; Mother's and Father's Day in May and June; July Fourth; September's Labor Day; October's Halloween; November's Thanksgiving; December's Christmas and Chanukah. The only exception is August, the one month with nary a day set aside for celebrations. Why should this month be void of holiday? It must be because August has always been the traditional month for family vacations and therefore needs no one special day for rest.

But let's not confuse vacations with holidays. Both should free us from daily routine and renew us through a change in our usual schedule. But vacations stress the freedom while holidays – in their original sense of Holy-Day – should stress renewal. As Americans, we have always been conscious of the fact that duty without freedom leads to tyranny, but freedom without duty leads to chaos. So if we ever begin to feel over-holidayed in America, especially when we're impatient for the banks and post offices to reopen, we should remember a sad truth nicely expressed by Mark Twain: "Pity the poor atheist; he can never celebrate a holiday."

A Canine Ishmael

By F. Anstey

'Tell me,' she said suddenly, with a pretty imperiousness that seemed to belong to her, 'are you fond of dogs?' How we arrived at the subject I forget now, but I know she had just been describing how a collie at a dog-show she had visited lately had suddenly thrown his forepaws round her neck in a burst of affection—a proceeding which, in my own mind (although I prudently kept this to myself), I considered less astonishing than she appeared to do.

For I had had the privilege of taking her in to dinner, and the meal had not reached a very advanced stage before I had come to the conclusion that she was the most charming, if not the loveliest, person I had ever met.

It was fortunate for me that I was honestly able to answer her question in a satisfactory manner, for, had it been otherwise, I doubt whether she would have deigned to bestow much more of her conversation upon me.

'Then I wonder,' she said next, meditatively, 'if you would care to hear about a dog that belonged to—to someone I know very well? Or would it bore you?'

I am very certain that if she had volunteered to relate the adventures of Telemachus, or the history of the Thirty Years' War, I should have accepted the proposal with a quite genuine gratitude. As it was, I made it sufficiently plain that I should care very much indeed to hear about that dog.

She paused for a moment to reject an unfortunate entrée (which I confess to doing my best to console), and then she began her story. I shall try to set it down as nearly as possible in her own words, although I cannot hope to convey the peculiar charm and interest that she gave it for me. It was not, I need hardly say, told all at once, but was subject to the inevitable interruptions which render a dinner-table intimacy so piquantly precarious.

'This dog,' she began quietly, without any air of beginning a story, 'this dog was called Pepper. He was not much to look at—rather a rough, mongrelly kind of animal; and he and a young man had kept house together for a long time, for the young man was a bachelor and lived in chambers by himself. He always used to say that he didn't like to get engaged to anyone, because he was sure it would put Pepper out so fearfully. However, he met somebody at last who made him forget about Pepper, and he proposed and was accepted—and then, you know,' she added, as a little dimple came in her cheek, 'he had to go home and break the news to the dog.'

She had just got to this point, when, taking advantage of a pause she made, the man on her other side (who was, I daresay, strictly within his rights, although I remember at the time considering him a pushing beast) struck in with some remark which she turned to answer, leaving me leisure to reflect.

I was feeling vaguely uncomfortable about this story; something, it would be hard to say what, in her way of mentioning Pepper's owner made me suspect that he was more than a mere acquaintance of hers.

Was it she, then, who was responsible for--? It was no business of mine, of course; I had never met her in my life till that evening—but I began to be impatient to hear the rest.

And at last she turned to me again: 'I hope you haven't forgotten that I was in the middle of a story. You haven't? And you would really like me to go on? Well, then—oh yes, when Pepper was told, he was naturally a little annoyed at first. I daresay he considered he ought to have been consulted previously. But, as soon as he had seen the lady, he withdrew all opposition—which his master declared was a tremendous load off his mind, for Pepper was rather a difficult dog, and slow as a rule to take strangers into his affections, a little snappy and surly, and very easily hurt or offended. Don't you know dogs who are sensitive like that? I do, and I'm always so sorry for them—they feel little things so much, and one never can find out what's the matter, and have it out with them! Sometimes it's shyness; once I had a dog who was quite painfully shy—self-consciousness it was really, I suppose, for he always fancied everybody was looking at him, and often when people were calling he would come and hide his face in the folds of my dress till they had gone—it was too ridiculous! But about Pepper. He was devoted to his new mistress from the very first. I am not sure that she was quite so struck with him, for he was not at all a lady's dog, and his manners had been very much neglected. Still, she came quite to like him in time; and when they were married, Pepper went with them for the honeymoon.'

'When they were married!' I glanced at the card which lay half-hidden by her plate. Surely Miss So-and-so was written on it?—yes, it was certainly 'Miss.' It was odd that such a circumstance should have increased my enjoyment of the story, perhaps—but it undoubtedly did.

'After the honeymoon,' my neighbour continued, 'they came to live in the new house, which was quite a tiny one, and Pepper was a very important personage in it indeed. He had his mistress all to himself for the greater part of most days, as his master had to be away in town; so she used to talk to him intimately, and tell him more than she would have thought of confiding to most people. Sometimes, when she thought there was no fear of callers coming, she would make him play, and this was quite a new sensation for Pepper, who was a serious-minded animal, and took very solemn views of life. At first he hadn't the faintest idea what was expected of him; it must have been rather like trying to romp with a parish beadle, he was so intensely respectable! But as soon as he once grasped the notion and understood that no liberty was intended, he lent himself to it readily enough and learnt to gambol quite creditably. Then he was made much of in all sorts of ways; she washed him twice a week with her very own hands—which his master would never have dreamt of doing—and she was always trying new ribbons on his complexion. That rather bored him at first, but it ended by making him a little conceited about his appearance. Altogether he was dearly fond of her, and I don't believe he had ever been happier in all his life than he was in those days. Only, unfortunately, it was all too good to last.'

Here I had to pass olives or something to somebody, and the other man, seeing his chance, and, to do him justice, with no idea that he was interrupting a story, struck in once more, so that the history of Pepper had to remain in abeyance for several minutes.

My uneasiness returned. Could there be a mistake about that name-card after all? Cards do get rearranged sometimes, and she seemed to know that young couple so very intimately. I tried to remember whether I had been introduced to her as a Miss or Mrs. So-and-so, but without success. There is some fatality which generally distracts one's attention at the critical moment of introduction, and in this case it was perhaps easily accounted for. My turn came again, and she took up her tale once more. 'I think when I left off I was saying that Pepper's happiness was too good to last. And so it was. For his mistress was ill, and, though he snuffed and scratched and whined at the door of her room for ever so long, they wouldn't let him in. But he managed to slip in one day somehow, and jumped up on her lap and licked her hands and face, and almost went out of his mind with joy at seeing her again. Only (I told you he was a sensitive dog) it gradually struck him that she was not quite so pleased to see him as usual—and and presently he found out the reason. There was another animal there, a new pet, which seemed to take up a good deal of her attention. Of course you guess what that was—but Pepper had never seen a baby before, and he took it as a personal slight and was dreadfully offended. He simply walked straight out of the room and downstairs to the kitchen, where he stayed for days.

'I don't think he enjoyed his sulk much, poor doggie; perhaps he had an idea that when they saw how much he took it to heart they would send the baby away. But as time went on and this didn't seem to occur to them, he decided to come out of the sulks and look over the matter, and he came back quite prepared to resume the old footing. Only everything was different. No one seemed to notice that he was in the room now, and his mistress never invited him to have a game; she even forgot to have him washed—and one of his peculiarities was that he had no objection to soap and warm water. The worst of it was, too, that before very long the baby followed him into the sitting-room, and, do what he could, he couldn't make the stupid little thing understand that it had no business there. If you think of it, a baby must strike a dog as a very inferior little animal: it can't bark (well, yes, it can howl), but it's no good whatever with rats, and yet everybody makes a tremendous fuss about it! The baby got all poor Pepper's bows now; and his mistress played games with it, though Pepper felt he could have done it ever so much better, but he was never allowed to join in.

So he used to lie on a rug and pretend he didn't mind, though, really, I'm certain he felt it horribly. I always believe, you know, that people never give dogs half credit enough for feeling things, don't you?

'Well, at last came the worst indignity of all: Pepper was driven from his rug—his own particular rug—to make room for the baby; and when he had got away into a corner to cry quietly, all by himself, that wretched baby came and crawled after him and pulled his tail!

'He always had been particular about his tail, and never allowed anybody to touch it but very intimate friends, and even then under protest, so you can imagine how insulted he felt.

'It was too much for him, and he lost the last scrap of temper he had. They said he bit the baby, and I'm afraid he did—though not enough really to hurt it; still, it howled fearfully, of course, and from that moment it was all over with poor Pepper—he was a ruined dog!

'When his master came home that evening he was told the whole story. Pepper's mistress said she would be ever so sorry to part with him, but, after his misbehaviour, she should never know a moment's peace until he was out of the house—it really wasn't safe for baby!

'And his master was sorry, naturally; but I suppose he was beginning rather to like the baby himself, and so the end of it was that Pepper had to go. They did all they could for him; found him a comfortable home, with a friend who was looking out for a good house-dog, and wasn't particular about breed, and, after that, they heard nothing of him for a long while. And, when they did hear, it was rather a bad report: the friend could do nothing with Pepper at all; he had to tie him up in the stable, and then he snapped at everyone who came near, and howled all night—they were really almost afraid of him.

'So when Pepper's mistress heard that, she felt more thankful than ever that the dog had been sent away, and tried to think no more about him. She had quite forgotten all about it, when, one day, a new nursemaid, who had taken the baby out for an airing, came back with a terrible account of a savage dog which had attacked them, and leaped up at the perambulator so persistently that it was as much as she could do to drive it away.

And even then Pepper's mistress did not associate the dog with him; she thought he had been destroyed long ago.

'But the next time the nurse went out with the baby she took a thick stick with her, in case the dog should come again. And no sooner had she lifted the perambulator over the step, than the dog did come again, exactly as if he had been lying in wait for them ever since outside the gate.

'The nurse was a strong country girl, with plenty of pluck, and as the dog came leaping and barking about in a very alarming way, she hit him as hard as she could on his head. The wonder is she did not kill him on the spot, and, as it was, the blow turned him perfectly giddy and silly for a time, and he ran round and round in a dazed sort of way—do you think you could lower that candle-shade just a little? Thanks!' she broke off suddenly, as I obeyed. 'Well, she was going to strike again, when her mistress rushed out, just in time to stop her. For, you see, she had been watching at the window, and although the poor beast was miserably thin, and rough, and neglected-looking, she knew at once that it must be Pepper, and that he was not in the least mad or dangerous, but only trying his best to make his peace with the baby. Very likely his dignity or his conscience or something wouldn't let him come back quite at once, you know; and perhaps he thought he had better get the baby on his side first. And then all at once, his mistress—I heard all this through her, of course—his mistress suddenly remembered how devoted Pepper had been to her, and how fond she had once been of him, and when she saw him standing, stupid and shivering, there, her heart softened to him, and she went to make it up with him, and tell him that he was forgiven and should come back and be her dog again, just as in the old days!'

Here she broke off for a moment. I did not venture to look at her, but I thought her voice trembled a little when she spoke again. 'I don't quite know why I tell you all this. There was a time when I never could bear the end of it myself,' she said; 'but I have begun, and I will finish now. Well, Pepper's mistress went towards him, and called him; but—whether he was still too dizzy to quite understand who she was, or whether his pride came uppermost again, poor dear! I don't know—but he gave her just one look (she says she will never forget it—never;

it went straight to her heart), and then he walked very slowly and deliberately away.

'She couldn't bear it; she followed; she felt she simply must make him understand how very, very sorry she was for him; but the moment he heard her he began to run faster and faster, until he was out of reach and out of sight, and she had to come back. I know she was crying bitterly by that time.'

'And he never came back again?' I asked, after a silence.

'Never again!' she said softly; 'that was the very last they ever saw or heard of him. And—and I've always loved every dog since for Pepper's sake!'

'I'm almost glad he did decline to come back,' I declared; 'it served his mistress right—she didn't deserve anything else!'

'Ah, I didn't want you to say that!' she protested; 'she never meant to be so unkind—it was all for the baby's sake!'

I was distinctly astonished, for all her sympathy in telling the story had seemed to lie in the other direction.

'You don't mean to say,' I cried involuntarily, 'that you can find any excuses for her? I did not expect you would take the baby's part!'

'But I did,' she confessed, with lowered eyes—'I did take the baby's part—it was all my doing that Pepper was sent away—I have been sorry enough for it since!'

It was her own story she had been telling at second-hand after all—and she was not Miss So-and-so! I had entirely forgotten the existence of any other members of the party but our two selves, but at the moment of this discovery—which was doubly painful—I was recalled by a general rustle to the fact that we were at a dinner-party, and that our hostess had just given the signal.

As I rose and drew back my chair to allow my neighbour to pass, she raised her eyes for a moment and said almost meekly:

'I was the baby, you see!'

The dog was created specially for children. He is the god of frolic. --- Henry Ward Beecher

The Dog's Commandments

By Christopher Morley

From a witless puppy I brought thee up: gave thee fire and food, and taught thee the self-respect of an honest dog. Hear, then, my commandments:

I am thy master: thou shalt have no other masters before me. Where I go, shalt thou follow; where I abide, tarry thou also.

My house is thy castle; thou shalt honor it; guard it with thy life if need be.

By daylight, suffer all that approach peaceably to enter without protest. But after nightfall thou shalt give tongue when men draw near.

Use not thy teeth on any man without good cause and intolerable provocation; and never on women or children.

Honor thy master and thy mistress, that thy days may be long in the land.

Thou shalt not consort with mongrels, nor with dogs that are common or unclean.

Thou shalt not steal. Thou shalt not feed upon refuse or stray bits: thy meat waits thee regularly in the kitchen.

Thou shalt not bury bones in the flower beds.

Cats are to be chased, but in sport only; seek not to devour them: their teeth and claws are deadly.

Thou shalt not snap at my neighbor, nor at his wife, nor his child, nor his manservant, nor his maidservant, nor his ox, nor his ass, nor do harm to aught that is his.

The drawing-room rug is not for thee, nor the sofa, nor the best armchair. Thou hast the porch and thy own kennel. But for the love I bear thee, there is always a corner for thee by the winter fire.

Meditate on these commandments day and night; so shalt thou be a dog of good breeding and an honor to thy master.

You'll notice in my essay I state "to read is to tiptoe into another's mind." Smith's story and Elizabeth Barrett Browning's poem convince us that great authors are even able to tiptoe within the wondrous minds of our canine companions.

Because my father owned a woman's hosiery store, I found myself employed during high school summer vacations at Midwestern Hosiery Company. Being able to call my boss 'Dad' had its advantages. My hours of work were basically from when I wanted to appear (10:00a.m. seemed a congenial hour) until Dad ran out of busy work and sent me home, much to the relief of both of us.

Dad had been a history major in college, and on one particularly slow day at work he told me a remarkable story about the history of hosiery. My father might have been a businessman at work, but he was a teacher at heart and loved sharing his stories and opinions with his three favorite students: my mother, my sister, and me. He began this lesson, as many teachers do, by asking a question: had I ever heard of Britain's King Ludd? Nope – but now I'll never forget him.

"King" Ludd was not a king at all, Dad began, but just a half-witted stocking maker named Ned Ludd who worked in Nottingham in 1800. The Industrial Revolution had just introduced sophisticated textile machinery in the area, causing great distress when the handicraftsmen throughout Northern England were dismissed and replaced by these new machines. Ned Ludd organized bands of English rioters who dubbed him "King." Wearing masks at night they smashed the new looms and frames in protest. By 1812 the riots spread throughout the country. Lord Byron gave a great speech in the House of Lords supporting Ned Ludd and his followers. But in 1813 there was a mass trial. Ned and many of his supporters were hanged – arms bound by the very stockings that the new machines had produced.

I've been thinking recently about my father's history lesson, especially as the new millennium continues to be called the Age of Information and continues to be praised for its technological advancements. Although the Ned Ludd episode has been pretty much forgotten in world history, it did produce a new word in 1812 which is still used today: Luddite – one who possesses a hatred of all technical innovation.

Alas, I must confess to standing nervously beneath this backward banner. This essay you are now reading was pen-scratched on a yellow legal pad and given directly to the newsletter editor. Not only was it not word-processed, it wasn't even typed. I can't say that I am proud of my computer illiteracy, but I do fancy my high-tech aversion as "quaint" rather than "pathetic."

In any case, what concerns me most as a Luddite is all this recent talk about the death of the printed book and its replacement by "plug-in books" on the internet's flickering screen. One futurist has opined that the book as we know it must die since "smearing ink on dead trees is the last smoke-stack industry."

Good gracious. Am I simply old-fashioned when I become horrified at the thought of reading a book being replaced by scrolling at a screen? Is curling up in bed with a good book going the way of the doornail and the dodo? Can't we celebrate the birth of a new technology without mourning the death of an old one?

Well, if loving the book itself makes me hopelessly low-tech, at least I find myself in very articulate company. When Omar Khayyam listed the joys of life, number one was "a book of verses underneath the bough." And before we consider writing the obituary for the book, let us heed John Milton's stern warning: "He who kills a man kills a reasonable creature in God's image, but he who destroys a book kills reason itself."

On those slow days at my father's store, it was a rare treat to be given one of his history lessons. Most often, when I was bored at work (and let me add that I was indeed most often bored at work) I banished the monotony by squirreling myself away behind a stack of hosiery boxes and then reading. Granted, the book I'd brought probably concerned the mysteries of the Hardy brothers rather than the mysteries of the brothers Karamazov. But regardless of the complexity, I was learning that culture offers few satisfactions more complete than reading and finishing a really, really great book. To read is to tiptoe inside another's mind. No legs are required, no computer either. You just need some "smeared ink on a dead tree" and an imagination ready to branch out endlessly with each leaf turned.

No one appreciates the very special genius of your conversation as much as the dog does. --- Christopher Morley

Another Dog

By Francis Hopkinson Smith

Do not tell me dogs cannot talk. I know better. I saw it all myself. It was at Sterzing, that most picturesque of all the Tyrolean villages on the Italian slope of the Brenner, with its long, single street, zigzagged like a straggling path in the snow, -- perhaps it was laid out in that way, -- and its little open square, with shrine and rude stone fountain, surrounded by women in short skirts and hobnailed shoes, dipping their buckets. On both sides of this street ran queer arcades sheltering shops, their doorways piled with cheap stuffs, fruit, farm implements, and the like, and at the far end, it was almost the last house in the town, stood the old inn, where you breakfast. Such an old, old inn! with swinging sign framed by fantastic iron work, and decorated with overflows of foaming ale in green mugs, crossed clay pipes, and little round dabs of yellow-brown cakes. There was a great archway, too, wide and high, with enormous, barn-like doors fronting on this straggling, zigzag, sabot-trodden street. Under this a cobble-stone pavement led to the door of the coffee-room and out to the stable beyond. These barn-like doors keep out the driving snows and the whirls of sleet and rain, and are slammed to behind horse, sleigh, and all, if not in the face, certainly in the very teeth of the winter gale, while the traveler disentangles his half-frozen legs at his leisure, almost within sight of the blazing fire of the coffee-room within.

Under this great archway, then, against one of these doors, his big paws just inside the shadow line, for it was not winter, but a brilliant summer morning, the grass all dusted with powdered diamonds, the sky a turquoise, the air a joy,--under this archway, I say, sat a big St. Bernard dog, squat on his haunches, his head well up, like a grenadier on guard. His eyes commanded the approaches down the road, up the road, and across the street; taking in the passing peddler with the tinware, and the girl with a basket strapped to her back, her fingers knitting for dear life, not to mention so unimportant an object as myself swinging down the road, my iron-shod alpenstock hammering the cobbles.

He made no objection to my entering, neither did he receive me with any show of welcome. There was no bounding forward, no wagging of the tail, no aimless walking around for a moment, and settling down in another spot; nor was there any sudden growl or forbidding look in the eye. None of these things occurred to him, for none of these things was part of his duty. The landlord would do the welcoming, the blue-shirted porter take my knapsack and show me the way to the coffee-room. His business was to sit still and guard that archway. Paying guests, and those known to the family,--yes! But stray mountain goats, chickens, inquisitive, pushing peddlers, pigs, and wandering dogs,--well, he would look out for these.

While the cutlets and coffee were being fried and boiled, I dragged a chair across the road and tilted it back out of the sun against the wall of a house. I, too, commanded a view down past the blacksmith shop, where they were heating a huge iron tire to clap on the hind wheel of a diligence, and up the street as far as the little square where the women were still clattering about on the cobbles, their buckets on their shoulders. This is how I happened to be watching the dog.

The more I looked at him, the more strongly did his personality impress me. The exceeding gravity of his demeanor! The dignified attitude! The quiet, silent reserve! The way he looked at you from under his eyebrows, not eagerly, nor furtively, but with a self-possessed, competent air, quite like a captain of a Cunarder scanning a horizon from the bridge, or a French gendarme, watching the shifting crowds from one of the little stone circles anchored out in the rush of the boulevards,--a look of authority backed by a sense of unlimited power. Then, too, there was such a dignified cut to his hairy chops as they drooped over his teeth beneath his black, stubby nose. His ears rose and fell easily, without undue haste or excitement when the sound of horses' hoofs put him on his guard, or a goat wandered too near. Yet one could see that he was not a meddlesome dog, nor a snarler, no running out and giving tongue at each passing object, not that kind of a dog at all! He was just a plain, substantial, well-mannered, dignified, self-respecting St. Bernard dog, who knew his place and kept it, who knew his duty and did it, and who would no more chase a cat than he would bite your legs in the dark. Put a cap with a gold band on his head and he would really have made an ideal concierge. Even without the band, he concentrated in his person all the superiority, the repose, and exasperating reticence of that necessary concomitant of Continental hotel life.

Suddenly I noticed a more eager expression on his face. One ear was unfurled, like a flag, and almost run to the masthead; the head was turned quickly down the road. A sound of wheels was heard below the shop. His dogship straightened himself and stood on four legs, his tail wagging slowly.

Another dog was coming.

A great Danish hound, with white eyes, black-and-tan ears, and tail as long and smooth as a policeman's night-club;--one of those sleek and shining dogs with powerful chest and knotted legs, a little bowed in front, black lips, and dazzling, fang-like teeth. He was spattered with brown spots, and sported a single white foot. Altogether, he was a dog of quality, of ancestry, of a certain position in his own land,--one who had clearly followed his master's mountain wagon to-day as much for love of adventure as anything else. A dog of parts, too, who could perhaps, hunt the wild boar, or give chase to the agile deer. He was certainly not an inn dog. He was rather a palace dog, a chateau, or a shooting-box dog, who, in his off moments, trotted behind hunting carts filled with guns, sportsmen in knee-breeches, or in front of landaus when my lady went an-airing.

And with all this, and quite naturally, he was a dog of breeding, who, while he insisted on his own rights, respected those of others. I saw this before he had spoken ten words to the concierge,--the St. Bernard dog, I mean. For he did talk to him, and the conversation was just as plain to me, tilted back against the wall, out of the sun, waiting for my cutlets and coffee, as if I had been a dog myself, and understood each word of it.

First, he walked up sideways, his tail wagging and straight out, like a patent towel-rack. Then he walked round the concierge, who followed his movements with becoming interest, wagging his own tail, straightening his forelegs, and sidling around him kindly, as befitted the stranger's rank and quality, but with a certain dog-independence of manner, preserving his own dignities while courteously passing the time of day, and intimating, by certain twists of his tail, that he felt quite sure his Excellency would like the air and scenery the farther he got up the pass,--all strange dogs did.

During this interchange of canine civilities, the landlord was helping out the two men, the companions of the dog. One was round and pudgy, the other lank and scrawny. Both were in knickerbockers, with green hats decorated with cock feathers and edelweiss. The blue-shirted porter carried in the bags and alpenstocks, closing the coffee-room door behind them.

Suddenly the strange dog, who had been beguiled by the courteous manner of the concierge, realized that his master had disappeared. The man had been hungry, no doubt, and half blinded by the glare of the sun. After the manner of his kind, he had dived into this shelter without a word to the dumb beast who had tramped behind his wheels, swallowing the dust his horses kicked up.

When the strange dog realized this,--I saw the instant the idea entered his mind, as I caught the sudden toss of the head,-- he glanced quickly about with that uneasy, anxious look that comes into the face of a dog when he discovers that he is adrift in a strange place without his master. What other face is so utterly miserable, and what eyes so pleading, the tears just under the lids, as the lost dog's?

Then it was beautiful to see the St. Bernard. With a sudden twist of the head he reassured the strange dog,--telling him, as plainly as could be, not to worry, the gentlemen were only inside, and would be out after breakfast. There was no mistaking what he said. It was done with a peculiar curving of the neck, a reassuring wag of the tail, a glance toward the coffee-room, and a few frolicsome, kittenish jumps, these last plainly indicating that as for himself the occasion was one of great hilarity, with absolutely no cause in it for anxiety. Then, if you could have seen that anxious look fade away from the face of the strange dog, the responsive, reciprocal wag of the night-club of a tail. If you could have caught the sudden peace that came into his eyes, and have seen him as he followed the concierge to the doorway, dropping his ears, and throwing himself beside him, looking up into his face, his tongue out, panting after the habit of his race, the white saliva dropping upon his paws.

Then followed a long talk, conducted in side glances, and punctuated with the quiet laughs of more slappings of tails on the cobbles, as the concierge listened to the adventures of the stranger, or matched them with funny experiences of his own.

Here a whistle from the coffee-room window startled them. Even so rude a being as a man is sometimes mindful of his dog. In an instant both concierge and stranger were on their feet, the concierge ready for whatever would turn up, the stranger trying to locate the sound and his master. Another whistle, and he was off, bounding down the road, looking wistfully at the windows, and rushing back bewildered. Suddenly it came to him that the short cut to his master lay through the archway.

Just here there was a change in the manner of the concierge. It was not gruff, nor savage, nor severe,--it was only firm and decided. With his tail still wagging, showing his kindness and willingness to oblige, but with spine rigid and hair bristling, he explained clearly and succinctly to that strange dog how absolutely impossible it would be for him to permit his crossing the archway. Up went the spine of the stranger, and out went his tail like a bar of steel, the feet braced, and the whole body taut as standing rigging. But the concierge kept on wagging his tail, though his hair still bristled,--saying as plainly as he could:--

"My dear sir, do not blame me. I assure you that nothing in the world would give me more pleasure than to throw the whole house open to you; but consider for a moment. My master puts me here to see that nobody enters the inn but those whom he wishes to see, and that all other live-stock, especially dogs, shall on no account be admitted." (This with head bent on one side and neck arched.) "Now, while I have the most distinguished consideration for your dogship" (tail wagging violently), "and would gladly oblige you, you must see that my honor is at stake" (spine more rigid), "and I feel assured that under the circumstances you will not press a request (low growl) which you must know would be impossible for me to grant."

And the strange dog, gentleman as he was, expressed himself as entirely satisfied with the very free and generous explanation. With tail wagging more violently than ever, he assured the concierge that he understood his position exactly. Then wheeling suddenly, he bounded down the road. Though convinced, he was still anxious.

Then the concierge gravely settled himself once more on his haunches in his customary place, his eyes commanding the view up and down and across the road, where I sat still tilted back in my chair waiting for my cutlets, his whole body at rest, his face expressive of that quiet content which comes from a sense of duties performed and honor untarnished.

But the stranger had duties, too; he must answer the whistle, and find his master. His search down the road being fruitless, he rushed back to the concierge, looking up into his face, his eyes restless and anxious.

"If it were inconsistent with his honor to permit him to cross the threshold, was there any other way he could get into the coffee-room?" This last with a low whine of uneasiness, and a toss of head.

"Yes, certainly," jumping to his feet, "why had he not mentioned it before? It would give him very great pleasure to show him the way to the side entrance." And the St. Bernard, everything wagging now, walked with the stranger to the corner, stopping stock still to point with his nose to the closed door.

Then the stranger bounded down with a scurry and plunge, nervously edging up to the door, wagging his tail, and with a low, anxious whine springing one side and another, his paws now on the sill, his nose at the crack, until the door was finally opened, and he dashed inside.

What happened in the coffee-room I do not know, for I could not see. I am willing, however, to wager that a dog of his loyalty, dignity, and sense of duty did just what a dog of quality would do. No awkward springing at his master's chest with his dusty paws leaving marks on his vest front; no rushing around chairs and tables in mad joy at being let in, alarming waitresses and children. Only a low whine and gurgle of delight, a rubbing of his cold nose against his master's hand, a low, earnest look up into his face, so frank, so trustful, a look that carried no reproach for being shut out, and only gratitude for being let in.

A moment more, and he was outside again, head in air, looking for his friend. Then a dash, and he was around by the archway, licking the concierge in the face, biting his neck, rubbing his nose under his forelegs, saying over and over again how deeply he thanked him,--how glad and proud he was of his acquaintance, and how delighted he would be if he came down to Vienna, or Milan, or wherever he did come from, so that he might return his courtesies in some way, and make his stay pleasant.

Just here the landlord called out that the cutlets and coffee were ready, and, man-like, I went in to breakfast.

It's no coincidence that man's best friend cannot talk. --- Anonymous

To Flush, My Dog

By Elizabeth Barrett Browning

Loving friend, the gift of one
Who her own true faith has run
Through thy lower nature,
Be my benediction said
With my hand upon thy head,
Gentle fellow-creature!

Like a lady's ringlets brown,
Flow thy silken ears adown
Either side demurely
Of thy silver-suited breast
Shining out from all the rest
Of thy body purely.

Darkly brown thy body is,
Till the sunshine striking this
Alchemise its dullness,
When the sleek curls manifold
Flash all over into gold
With a burnished fullness.

Underneath my stroking hand,
Startled eyes of hazel bland
Kindling, growing larger,
Up thou leapest with a spring,
Full of prank and curveting,
Leaping like a charger.

Leap! thy broad tail waves a light,
Leap! thy slender feet are bright,
Canopied in fringes;
Leap! those tasselled ears of thine

Flicker strangely, fair and fine
Down their golden inches.

Yet, my pretty, sportive friend,
Little is't to such an end
That I praise thy rareness;
Other dogs may be thy peers
Haply in these drooping ears
And this glossy fairness.

But of thee it shall be said,
This dog watched beside a bed
Day and night unweary,
Watched within a curtained room
Where no sunbeam brake the gloom
Round the sick and dreary.

Roses, gathered for a vase,
In that chamber died apace,
Beam and breeze resigning;
This dog only, waited on,
Knowing that when light is gone
Love remains for shining.

Other dogs in thymy dew
Tracked the hares and followed through
Sunny moor or meadow;
This dog only, crept and crept
Next a languid cheek that slept,
Sharing in the shadow.

Other dogs of loyal cheer
Bounded at the whistle clear,
Up the woodside hieing;
This dog only, watched in reach
Of a faintly uttered speech
Or a louder sighing.

And if one or two quick tears
Dropped upon his glossy ears

Or a sigh came double,
Up he sprang in eager haste,
Fawning, fondling, breathing fast,
In a tender trouble.

And this dog was satisfied
If a pale thin hand would glide
Down his dewlaps sloping, --
Which he pushed his nose within,
After, -- platforming his chin
On the palm left open.

This dog, if a friendly voice
Call him now to blither choice
Than such chamber-keeping,
"Come out!" praying from the door, --
Presseth backward as before,
Up against me leaping.

Therefore to this dog will I,
Tenderly not scornfully,
Render praise and favor:
With my hand upon his head,
Is my benediction said
Therefore and forever.

And because he loves me so,
Better than his kind will do
Often man or woman,
Give I back more love again
Than dogs often take of men,
Leaning from my Human.

Blessings on thee, dog of mine,
Pretty collars make thee fine,
Sugared milk make fat thee!
Pleasures wag on in thy tail,
Hands of gentle motion fail
Nevermore, to pat thee.

Downy pillow take thy head,
Silken coverlid bestead,
Sunshine help thy sleeping!
No fly's buzzing wake thee up,
No man break thy purple cup
Set for drinking deep in.

Whiskered cats arointed flee,
Sturdy stoppers keep from thee
Cologne distillations;
Nuts lie in thy path for stones,
And thy feast-day macaroons
Turn to daily rations!

Mock I thee, in wishing weal? --
Tears are in my eyes to feel
Thou art made so straitly,
Blessing needs must straiten too, --
Little canst thou joy or do,
Thou who lovest greatly.

Yet be blessed to the height
Of all good and all delight
Pervious to thy nature;
Only loved beyond that line,
With a love that answers thine,
Loving fellow-creature!

Both my essay and Chekhov's KASHTANKA deal with lively, lower-middle class European families. And both demonstrate the unique sense of security, humanity, and humility that reside there.

It's odd how a chance disappointment can direct your life toward an unexpected attainment. It certainly happened to me with my initial infatuation with the works of Charles Dickens. I was living in Los Angeles, pursuing my doctoral degree at UCLA. Actually, I was living in the dreadful city of Burbank, miles from the campus in an apartment that had only its low rent to recommend it to a poor graduate student.

A new French restaurant had opened down the street, and flyers had been put in neighboring mailboxes advertising a free gala first evening at which exotic desserts would be served. I had been studying all day for a Victorian literature final examination and needed a break and a snack; the invitation provided both so I walked down to "Les Pyrenees." I was ushered to a long table with other customers. The proprietor announced that our waiter would soon be bringing an "array of delectables."

For the next twenty minutes, we watched waiters occasionally snail past, lugging heavy trays and heavier attitudes. None stopped, nor did there seem any likelihood of attracting their attention; it put me in mind of Ogden Nash's wonderful *Epitaph for a Waiter* – "By and by/God caught his eye." Finally a tired man old enough to have been a founder of the city of Burbank deposited a small plate in front of each of us and muttered: "Enjoy your mousse and soufflé" with a tone of such ennui that it sounded more like a dare than a request.

Both desserts, though soft and sweet, lacked any allure or panache. They were as pretentious and soulless as the man who delivered them. I returned to my apartment sugared but surly and not at all eager to read *A Christmas Carol*, one of the works on the final exam the next day. As I started to read the story, it was so late and the tale so familiar that I dozed a bit and was about to call it a night when one quite famous passage startled me. It was the entrance of Mrs. Cratchit with the Christmas pudding "like a speckled cannon-ball, so hard and firm, blazing in half of half-a-quartern of ignited brandy and bedight with Christmas holly stuck into the top."

I was struck by the fact that this most delightful and famous dessert in all of Dickens was actually a poor cousin of the ostentatious soufflé and mousse I'd indulged in earlier. They, too, in spite of their fancy French names, were mere puddings – defined as "boiled or baked soft food with a cereal base." But Dickens made his humble dessert immortal by uniquely comparing it to a speckled cannon-ball and then adding that it was with holly bedight – an archaic term meaning "adorned" but somehow connoting an almost religious glow. Though my stomach was glutted with mediocre mousse and soufflé, I went to bed that night tasting and savoring the Christmas pudding that never existed except in Dickens dazzling imagination.

As I read more and more Dickens, I found more and more puddings in his novels. Because Dickens peoples his works with so many poor characters, there seemed to be more "suet puddings" than any other kind. *Suet* is the hard fat above the kidneys in beef and mutton used not only for puddings but in soap and candles as well. Only a Dickens could make this ghastly ingredient sound luscious, but he was indeed up for the challenge. Dickens went into great detail about how this pudding was wrapped in a dish towel hanging from a copper stick to steam over a pot of boiling water in the kitchen. The scene he creates is one of enchanting coziness with the humble family chattering away as they eagerly await the finished dessert. With Dickensian alchemy, he transforms a pudding based on mutton kidney fat into a soft, sweet, creamy loveliness that causes his characters and his readers to smack their lips.

I have always admired the humanity, humility, and humor of Dickens' characters who came from this lower-middle class that the English call "shabby genteel." Thanks to his own father's prodigality, Dickens himself grew up in a family equally poor and humble. And I think Dickens may have decided that the pudding was the perfect symbol for the sweetness and comfort that can still reside within families of reduced circumstances. As a dessert, it is the original humble pie, a thrifty way to recycle the day-old bread and cake that became the basis for most English puddings (including the humbly named 'trifle'). And what could be a more suitable national dessert than the pudding since it embraces all those ingredients we think of as uniquely and divinely English: clotted creams, fresh berries, currant jellies, and lemon curd?

It was Miguel Cervantes in *Don Quixote* in 1605 who first penned the now famous phrase: "The proof of the pudding is in the eating." That proverb proved equally true to me at the disappointing French restaurant and at my desk an hour later reading *A Christmas Carol* and being introduced to the inspired humanity of Charles Dickens.

Kashtanka

By Anton Chekhov

I.

Misbehaviour

A YOUNG dog, a reddish mongrel, between a dachshund and a "yard-dog," very like a fox in face, was running up and down the pavement looking uneasily from side to side. From time to time she stopped and, whining and lifting first one chilled paw and then another, tried to make up her mind how it could have happened that she was lost.

She remembered very well how she had passed the day, and how, in the end, she had found herself on this unfamiliar pavement.

The day had begun by her master Luka Alexandritch's putting on his hat, taking something wooden under his arm wrapped up in a red handkerchief, and calling: "Kashtanka, come along!"

Hearing her name the mongrel had come out from under the work-table, where she slept on the shavings, stretched herself voluptuously and run after her master. The people Luka Alexandritch worked for lived a very long way off, so that, before he could get to any one of them, the carpenter had several times to step into a tavern to fortify himself. Kashtanka remembered that on the way she had behaved extremely improperly. In her delight that she was being taken for a walk she jumped about, dashed barking after the trains, ran into yards, and chased other dogs. The carpenter was continually losing sight of her, stopping, and angrily shouting at her. Once he had even, with an expression of fury in his face, taken her fox-like ear in his fist, smacked her, and said emphatically: "Pla-a-ague take you, you pest!"

After having left the work where it had been bespoken, Luka Alexandritch went into his sister's and there had something to eat and drink; from his sister's he had gone to see a bookbinder he knew; from the bookbinder's to a tavern, from the tavern to another crony's, and so on. In short, by the time Kashtanka found herself on the unfamiliar pavement, it was getting dusk, and the carpenter was as drunk as a cobbler. He was waving his arms and, breathing heavily, muttered:

"In sin my mother bore me! Ah, sins, sins! Here now we are walking along the street and looking at the street lamps, but when we die, we shall burn in a fiery Gehenna. . . ."

Or he fell into a good-natured tone, called Kashtanka to him, and said to her: "You, Kashtanka, are an insect of a creature, and nothing else. Beside a man, you are much the same as a joiner beside a cabinet-maker. . . ."

While he talked to her in that way, there was suddenly a burst of music. Kashtanka looked round and saw that a regiment of soldiers was coming straight towards her. Unable to endure the music, which unhinged her nerves, she turned round and round and wailed. To her great surprise, the carpenter, instead of being frightened, whining and barking, gave a broad grin, drew himself up to attention, and saluted with all his five fingers. Seeing that her master did not protest, Kashtanka whined louder than ever, and dashed across the road to the opposite pavement.

When she recovered herself, the band was not playing and the regiment was no longer there. She ran across the road to the spot where she had left her master, but alas, the carpenter was no longer there. She dashed forward, then back again and ran across the road once more, but the carpenter seemed to have vanished into the earth. Kashtanka began sniffing the pavement, hoping to find her master by the scent of his tracks, but some wretch had been that way just before in new rubber galoshes, and now all delicate scents were mixed with an acute stench of India-rubber, so that it was impossible to make out anything.

Kashtanka ran up and down and did not find her master, and meanwhile it had got dark. The street lamps were lighted on both sides of the road, and lights appeared in the windows. Big, fluffy snowflakes were falling and painting white the pavement, the horses' backs and the cabmen's caps, and the darker the evening grew the whiter were all these objects. Unknown customers kept walking incessantly to and fro, obstructing her field of vision and shoving against her with their feet. (All mankind Kashtanka divided into two uneven parts: masters and customers; between them there was an essential difference: the first had the right to beat her, and the second she had the right to nip by the calves of their legs.) These customers were hurrying off somewhere and paid no attention to her.

When it got quite dark, Kashtanka was overcome by despair and horror. She huddled up in an entrance and began whining piteously. The long day's journeying with Luka Alexandritch had exhausted her, her ears and her paws were freezing, and, what was more, she was terribly hungry. Only twice in the whole day had she tasted a morsel: she had eaten a little paste at the bookbinder's, and in one of the taverns she had found a sausage skin on the floor, near the counter—that was all. If she had been a human being she would have certainly thought: "No, it is impossible to live like this! I must shoot myself!"

II.

A Mysterious Stranger

But she thought of nothing, she simply whined. When her head and back were entirely plastered over with the soft feathery snow, and she had sunk into a painful doze of exhaustion, all at once the door of the entrance clicked, creaked, and struck her on the side. She jumped up. A man belonging to the class of customers came out. As Kashtanka whined and got under his feet, he could not help noticing her. He bent down to her and asked:

"Doggy, where do you come from? Have I hurt you? O, poor thing, poor thing. . . . Come, don't be cross, don't be cross. . . . I am sorry."

Kashtanka looked at the stranger through the snowflakes that hung on her eyelashes, and saw before her a short, fat little man, with a plump, shaven face wearing a top hat and a fur coat that swung open.

"What are you whining for?" he went on, knocking the snow off her back with his fingers. "Where is your master? I suppose you are lost? Ah, poor doggy! What are we going to do now?"

Catching in the stranger's voice a warm, cordial note, Kashtanka licked his hand, and whined still more pitifully.

"Oh, you nice funny thing!" said the stranger. "A regular fox! Well, there's nothing for it, you must come along with me! Perhaps you will be of use for something. . . . Well!"

He clicked with his lips, and made a sign to Kashtanka with his hand, which could only mean one thing: "Come along!" Kashtanka went.

Not more than half an hour later she was sitting on the floor in a big, light room, and, leaning her head against her side, was looking with tenderness and curiosity at the stranger who was sitting at the table, dining. He ate and threw pieces to her. . . . At first he gave her bread and the green rind of cheese, then a piece of meat, half a pie and chicken bones, while through hunger she ate so quickly that she had not time to distinguish the taste, and the more she ate the more acute was the feeling of hunger.

"Your masters don't feed you properly," said the stranger, seeing with what ferocious greediness she swallowed the morsels without munching them. "And how thin you are! Nothing but skin and bones. . . ."

Kashtanka ate a great deal and yet did not satisfy her hunger, but was simply stupefied with eating. After dinner she lay down in the middle of the room, stretched her legs and, conscious of an agreeable weariness all over her body, wagged her tail. While her new master, lounging in an easy-chair, smoked a cigar, she wagged her tail and considered the question, whether it was better at the stranger's or at the carpenter's. The stranger's surroundings were poor and ugly; besides the easy-chairs, the sofa, the lamps and the rugs, there was nothing, and the room seemed empty. At the carpenter's the whole place was stuffed full of things: he had a table, a bench, a heap of shavings, planes, chisels, saws, a cage with a goldfinch, a basin. . . . The stranger's room smelt of nothing, while there was always a thick fog in the carpenter s room, and a glorious smell of glue, varnish, and shavings. On the other hand, the stranger had one great superiority—he gave her a great deal to eat and, to do him full justice, when Kashtanka sat facing the table and looking wistfully at him, he did not once hit or kick her, and did not once shout: "Go away, damned brute!"

When he had finished his cigar her new master went out, and a minute later came back holding a little mattress in his hands.

"Hey, you dog, come here!" he said, laying the mattress in the corner near the dog. "Lie down here, go to sleep!"

Then he put out the lamp and went away. Kashtanka lay down on the mattress and shut her eyes; the sound of a bark rose from the street, and she would have liked to answer it, but all at once she was overcome with unexpected melancholy. She thought of Luka Alexandritch, of his son Fedyushka, and her snug little place under the bench. . . . She remembered on the long winter evenings, when the carpenter was planing or reading the paper aloud, Fedyushka usually played with her. . . . He used to pull her from under the bench by her hind legs, and play such tricks with her, that she saw green before her eyes, and ached in every joint. He would make her walk on her hind legs, use her as a bell, that is, shake her violently by the tail so that she squealed and barked, and give her tobacco to sniff. . . . The following trick was particularly agonising: Fedyushka would tie a piece of meat to a thread and give it to Kashtanka, and then, when she had swallowed it he would, with a loud laugh, pull it back again from her stomach, and the more lurid were her memories the more loudly and miserably Kashtanka whined.

But soon exhaustion and warmth prevailed over melancholy. She began to fall asleep. Dogs ran by in her imagination: among them a shaggy old poodle, whom she had seen that day in the street with a white patch on his eye and tufts of wool by his nose. Fedyushka ran after the poodle with a chisel in his hand, then all at once he too was covered with shaggy wool, and began merrily barking beside Kashtanka. Kashtanka and he goodnaturedly sniffed each other's noses and merrily ran down the street. . . .

III.

New and Very Agreeable Acquaintances

When Kashtanka woke up it was already light, and a sound rose from the street, such as only comes in the day-time. There was not a soul in the room. Kashtanka stretched, yawned and, cross and ill-humoured, walked about the room. She sniffed the corners and the furniture, looked into the passage and found nothing of interest there. Besides the door that led into the passage there was another door. After thinking a little Kashtanka scratched on it with both paws, opened it, and went into the adjoining room. Here on the bed, covered with a rug, a customer, in whom she recognised the stranger of yesterday, lay asleep.

"Rrrrr . . . " she growled, but recollecting yesterday's dinner, wagged her tail, and began sniffing.

She sniffed the stranger's clothes and boots and thought they smelt of horses. In the bedroom was another door, also closed. Kashtanka scratched at the door, leaned her chest against it, opened it, and was instantly aware of a strange and very suspicious smell. Foreseeing an unpleasant encounter, growling and looking about her, Kashtanka walked into a little room with a dirty wallpaper and drew back in alarm. She saw something surprising and terrible. A grey gander came straight towards her, hissing, with its neck bowed down to the floor and its wings outspread. Not far from him, on a little mattress, lay a white tomcat; seeing Kashtanka, he jumped up, arched his back, wagged his tail with his hair standing on end and he, too, hissed at her. The dog was frightened in earnest, but not caring to betray her alarm, began barking loudly and dashed at the cat. . . . The cat arched his back more than ever, mewed and gave Kashtanka a smack on the head with his paw. Kashtanka jumped back, squatted on all four paws, and craning her nose towards the cat, went off into loud, shrill barks; meanwhile the gander came up behind and gave her a painful peck in the back. Kashtanka leapt up and dashed at the gander.

"What's this?" They heard a loud angry voice, and the stranger came into the room in his dressing-gown, with a cigar between his teeth. "What's the meaning of this? To your places!"

He went up to the cat, flicked him on his arched back, and said:

"Fyodor Timofeyitch, what's the meaning of this? Have you got up a fight? Ah, you old rascal! Lie down!"

And turning to the gander he shouted: "Ivan Ivanitch, go home!"

The cat obediently lay down on his mattress and closed his eyes. Judging from the expression of his face and whiskers, he was displeased with himself for having lost his temper and got into a fight.

Kashtanka began whining resentfully, while the gander craned his neck and began saying something rapidly, excitedly, distinctly, but quite unintelligibly.

"All right, all right," said his master, yawning. "You must live in peace and friendship." He stroked Kashtanka and went on: "And you, redhair, don't be frightened. . . . They are capital company, they won't annoy you. Stay, what are we to call you? You can't go on without a name, my dear."

The stranger thought a moment and said: "I tell you what . . . you shall be Auntie. . . . Do you understand? Auntie!"

And repeating the word "Auntie" several times he went out. Kashtanka sat down and began watching. The cat sat motionless on his little mattress, and pretended to be asleep. The gander, craning his neck and stamping, went on talking rapidly and excitedly about something. Apparently it was a very clever gander; after every long tirade, he always stepped back with an air of wonder and made a show of being highly delighted with his own speech. . . . Listening to him and answering "R-r-r-r," Kashtanka fell to sniffing the corners. In one of the corners she found a little trough in which she saw some soaked peas and a sop of rye crusts. She tried the peas; they were not nice; she tried the sopped bread and began eating it. The gander was not at all offended that the strange dog was eating his food, but, on the contrary, talked even more excitedly, and to show his confidence went to the trough and ate a few peas himself.

IV.

Marvels on a Hurdle

A little while afterwards the stranger came in again, and brought a strange thing with him like a hurdle, or like the figure II. On the crosspiece on the top of this roughly made wooden frame hung a bell, and a pistol was also tied to it; there were strings from the tongue of the bell, and the trigger of the pistol. The stranger put the frame in the middle of the room, spent a long time tying and untying something, then looked at the gander and said: "Ivan Ivanitch, if you please!"

The gander went up to him and stood in an expectant attitude.

"Now then," said the stranger, "let us begin at the very beginning. First of all, bow and make a curtsey! Look sharp!"

Ivan Ivanitch craned his neck, nodded in all directions, and scraped with his foot.

"Right. Bravo. . . . Now die!"

The gander lay on his back and stuck his legs in the air. After performing a few more similar, unimportant tricks, the stranger suddenly clutched at his head, and assuming an expression of horror, shouted: "Help! Fire! We are burning!"

Ivan Ivanitch ran to the frame, took the string in his beak, and set the bell ringing.

The stranger was very much pleased. He stroked the gander's neck and said:

"Bravo, Ivan Ivanitch! Now pretend that you are a jeweller selling gold and diamonds. Imagine now that you go to your shop and find thieves there. What would you do in that case?"

The gander took the other string in his beak and pulled it, and at once a deafening report was heard. Kashtanka was highly delighted with the bell ringing, and the shot threw her into so much ecstasy that she ran round the frame barking.

"Auntie, lie down!" cried the stranger; "be quiet!"

Ivan Ivanitch's task was not ended with the shooting. For a whole hour afterwards the stranger drove the gander round him on a cord, cracking a whip, and the gander had to jump over barriers and through hoops; he had to rear, that is, sit on his tail and wave his legs in the air. Kashtanka could not take her eyes off Ivan Ivanitch, wriggled with delight, and several times fell to running after him with shrill barks. After exhausting the gander and himself, the stranger wiped the sweat from his brow and cried:

"Marya, fetch Havronya Ivanovna here!"

A minute later there was the sound of grunting. Kashtanka growled, assumed a very valiant air, and to be on the safe side, went nearer to the stranger. The door opened, an old woman looked in, and, saying something, led in a black and very ugly sow. Paying no attention to Kashtanka's growls, the sow lifted up her little hoof and grunted good-humouredly. Apparently it was very agreeable to her to see her master, the cat, and Ivan Ivanitch. When she went up to the cat and gave him a light tap on the stomach with her hoof, and then made some remark to the gander, a great deal of good-nature was expressed in her movements, and the quivering of her tail. Kashtanka realised at once that to growl and bark at such a character was useless.

The master took away the frame and cried. "Fyodor Timofeyitch, if you please!"

The cat stretched lazily, and reluctantly, as though performing a duty, went up to the sow.

"Come, let us begin with the Egyptian pyramid," began the master. He spent a long time explaining something, then gave the word of command, "One . . . two . . . three!" At the word "three" Ivan Ivanitch flapped his wings and jumped on to the sow's back. . . . When, balancing himself with his wings and his neck, he got a firm foothold on the bristly back, Fyodor Timofeyitch listlessly and lazily, with manifest disdain, and with an air of scorning his art and not caring a pin for it, climbed on to the sow's back, then reluctantly mounted on to the gander, and stood on his hind legs. The result was what the stranger called the Egyptian pyramid. Kashtanka yapped with delight, but at that moment the old cat yawned and, losing his balance, rolled off the gander. Ivan Ivanitch lurched and fell off too. The stranger shouted, waved his hands, and began explaining something again. After spending an hour over the pyramid their indefatigable master proceeded to teach Ivan Ivanitch to ride on the cat, then began to teach the cat to smoke, and so on.

The lesson ended in the stranger's wiping the sweat off his brow and going away. Fyodor Timofeyitch gave a disdainful sniff, lay down on his mattress, and closed his eyes; Ivan Ivanitch went to the trough, and the pig was taken away by the old woman. Thanks to the number of her new impressions, Kashtanka hardly noticed how the day passed, and in the evening she was installed with her mattress in the room with the dirty wall-paper, and spent the night in the society of Fyodor Timofeyitch and the gander.

V.

Talent! Talent!

A month passed.

Kashtanka had grown used to having a nice dinner every evening, and being called Auntie. She had grown used to the stranger too, and to her new companions. Life was comfortable and easy.

Every day began in the same way. As a rule, Ivan Ivanitch was the first to wake up, and at once went up to Auntie or to the cat, twisting his neck, and beginning to talk excitedly and persuasively, but, as before, unintelligibly. Sometimes he would crane up his head in the air and utter a long monologue. At first Kashtanka thought he talked so much because he was very clever, but after a little time had passed, she lost all her respect for him; when he went up to her with his long speeches she no longer wagged her tail, but treated him as a tiresome chatterbox, who would not let anyone sleep and, without the slightest ceremony, answered him with

"R-r-r-r!"

Fyodor Timofeyitch was a gentleman of a very different sort. When he woke he did not utter a sound, did not stir, and did not even open his eyes. He would have been glad not to wake, for, as was evident, he was not greatly in love with life. Nothing interested him, he showed an apathetic and nonchalant attitude to everything, he disdained everything and, even while eating his delicious dinner, sniffed contemptuously.

When she woke Kashtanka began walking about the room and sniffing the corners. She and the cat were the only ones allowed to go all over the flat; the gander had not the right to cross the threshold of the room with the dirty wallpaper, and Havronya Ivanovna lived somewhere in a little outhouse in the yard and made her appearance only during the lessons. Their master got up late, and immediately after drinking his tea began teaching them their tricks. Every day the frame, the whip, and the hoop were brought in, and every day almost the same performance took place. The lesson lasted three or four hours, so that sometimes Fyodor Timofeyitch was so tired that he staggered about like a drunken man, and Ivan Ivanitch opened his beak and breathed heavily, while their master became red in the face and could not mop the sweat from his brow fast enough.

The lesson and the dinner made the day very interesting, but the evenings were tedious. As a rule, their master went off somewhere in the evening and took the cat and the gander with him. Left alone, Auntie lay down on her little mattress and began to feel sad.

Melancholy crept on her imperceptibly and took possession of her by degrees, as darkness does of a room. It began with the dog's losing every inclination to bark, to eat, to run about the rooms, and even to look at things; then vague figures, half dogs, half human beings, with countenances attractive, pleasant, but incomprehensible, would appear in her imagination; when they came Auntie wagged her tail, and it seemed to her that she had somewhere, at some time, seen them and loved them. And as she dropped asleep, she always felt that those figures smelt of glue, shavings, and varnish.

When she had grown quite used to her new life, and from a thin, long mongrel, had changed into a sleek, well-groomed dog, her master looked at her one day before the lesson and said:

"It's high time, Auntie, to get to business. You have kicked up your heels in idleness long enough. I want to make an artiste of you. . . . Do you want to be an artiste?"

And he began teaching her various accomplishments. At the first lesson he taught her to stand and walk on her hind legs, which she liked extremely. At the second lesson she had to jump on her hind legs and catch some sugar, which her teacher held high above her head. After that, in the following lessons she danced, ran tied to a cord, howled to music, rang the bell, and fired the pistol, and in a month could successfully replace Fyodor Timofeyitch in the "Egyptian Pyramid." She learned very eagerly and was pleased with her own success; running with her tongue out on the cord, leaping through the hoop, and riding on old Fyodor Timofeyitch, gave her the greatest enjoyment. She accompanied every successful trick with a shrill, delighted bark, while her teacher wondered, was also delighted, and rubbed his hands.

"It's talent! It's talent!" he said. "Unquestionable talent! You will certainly be successful!"

And Auntie grew so used to the word talent, that every time her master pronounced it, she jumped up as if it had been her name.

VI.

An Uneasy Night

Auntie had a doggy dream that a porter ran after her with a broom, and she woke up in a fright.

It was quite dark and very stuffy in the room. The fleas were biting. Auntie had never been afraid of darkness before, but now, for some reason, she felt frightened and inclined to bark.

Her master heaved a loud sigh in the next room, then soon afterwards the sow grunted in her sty, and then all was still again. When one thinks about eating one's heart grows lighter, and Auntie began thinking how that day she had stolen the leg of a chicken from Fyodor Timofeyitch, and had hidden it in the drawing-room, between the cupboard and the wall, where there were a great many spiders' webs and a great deal of dust. Would it not be as well to go now and look whether the chicken leg were still there or not? It was very possible that her master had found it and eaten it. But she must not go out of the room before morning, that was the rule. Auntie shut her eyes to go to sleep as quickly as possible, for she knew by experience that the sooner you go to sleep the sooner the morning comes. But all at once there was a strange scream not far from her which made her start and jump up on all four legs. It was Ivan Ivanitch, and his cry was not babbling and persuasive as usual, but a wild, shrill, unnatural scream like the squeak of a door opening. Unable to distinguish anything in the darkness, and not understanding what was wrong, Auntie felt still more frightened and growled: "R-r-r-r. . . ."

Some time passed, as long as it takes to eat a good bone; the scream was not repeated. Little by little Auntie's uneasiness passed off and she began to doze. She dreamed of two big black dogs with tufts of last year's coat left on their haunches and sides; they were eating out of a big basin some swill, from which there came a white steam and a most appetising smell; from time to time they looked round at Auntie, showed their teeth and growled: "We are not going to give you any!" But a peasant in a fur-coat ran out of the house and drove them away with a whip; then Auntie went up to the basin and began eating, but as soon as the peasant went out of the gate, the two black dogs rushed at her growling, and all at once there was again a shrill scream.

"K-gee! K-gee-gee!" cried Ivan Ivanitch.

Auntie woke, jumped up and, without leaving her mattress, went off into a yelping bark. It seemed to her that it was not Ivan Ivanitch that was screaming but someone else, and for some reason the sow again grunted in her sty.

Then there was the sound of shuffling slippers, and the master came into the room in his dressing-gown with a candle in his hand. The flickering light danced over the dirty wallpaper and the ceiling, and chased away the darkness. Auntie saw that there was no stranger in the room. Ivan Ivanitch was sitting on the floor and was not asleep. His wings were spread out and his beak was open, and altogether he looked as though he were very tired and thirsty. Old Fyodor Timofeyitch was not asleep either. He, too, must have been awakened by the scream.

"Ivan Ivanitch, what's the matter with you?" the master asked the gander. "Why are you screaming? Are you ill?"

The gander did not answer. The master touched him on the neck, stroked his back, and said: "You are a queer chap. You don't sleep yourself, and you don't let other people. . . ."

When the master went out, carrying the candle with him, there was darkness again. Auntie felt frightened. The gander did not scream, but again she fancied that there was some stranger in the room. What was most dreadful was that this stranger could not be bitten, as he was unseen and had no shape. And for some reason she thought that something very bad would certainly happen that night. Fyodor Timofeyitch was uneasy too.

Auntie could hear him shifting on his mattress, yawning and shaking his head.

Somewhere in the street there was a knocking at a gate and the sow grunted in her sty. Auntie began to whine, stretched out her front paws and laid her head down upon them. She fancied that in the knocking at the gate, in the grunting of the sow, who was for some reason awake, in the darkness and the stillness, there was something as miserable and dreadful as in Ivan Ivanitch's scream. Everything was in agitation and anxiety, but why? Who was the stranger who could not be seen? Then two dim flashes of green gleamed for a minute near Auntie. It was Fyodor Timofeyitch, for the first time of their whole acquaintance coming up to her. What did he want? Auntie licked his paw, and not asking why he had come, howled softly and on various notes.

"K-gee!" cried Ivan Ivanitch, "K-g-ee!"

The door opened again and the master came in with a candle.

The gander was sitting in the same attitude as before, with his beak open, and his wings spread out, his eyes were closed.

"Ivan Ivanitch!" his master called him.

The gander did not stir. His master sat down before him on the floor, looked at him in silence for a minute, and said:

"Ivan Ivanitch, what is it? Are you dying? Oh, I remember now, I remember!" he cried out, and clutched at his head. "I know why it is! It's because the horse stepped on you today! My God! My God!"

Auntie did not understand what her master was saying, but she saw from his face that he, too, was expecting something dreadful. She stretched out her head towards the dark window, where it seemed to her some stranger was looking in, and howled.

"He is dying, Auntie!" said her master, and wrung his hands. "Yes, yes, he is dying! Death has come into your room. What are we to do?"

Pale and agitated, the master went back into his room, sighing and shaking his head. Auntie was afraid to remain in the darkness, and followed her master into his bedroom. He sat down on the bed and repeated several times: "My God, what's to be done?"

Auntie walked about round his feet, and not understanding why she was wretched and why they were all so uneasy, and trying to understand, watched every movement he made. Fyodor Timofeyitch, who rarely left his little mattress, came into the master's bedroom too, and began rubbing himself against his feet. He shook his head as though he wanted to shake painful thoughts out of it, and kept peeping suspiciously under the bed.

The master took a saucer, poured some water from his washstand into it, and went to the gander again.

"Drink, Ivan Ivanitch!" he said tenderly, setting the saucer before him; "drink, darling."

But Ivan Ivanitch did not stir and did not open his eyes. His master bent his head down to the saucer and dipped his beak into the water, but the gander did not drink, he spread his wings wider than ever, and his head remained lying in the saucer.

"No, there's nothing to be done now," sighed his master. "It's all over. Ivan Ivanitch is gone!"

And shining drops, such as one sees on the windowpane when it rains, trickled down his cheeks. Not understanding what was the matter, Auntie and Fyodor Timofeyitch snuggled up to him and looked with horror at the gander.

"Poor Ivan Ivanitch!" said the master, sighing mournfully. "And I was dreaming I would take you in the spring into the country, and would walk with you on the green grass. Dear creature, my good comrade, you are no more! How shall I do without you now?"

It seemed to Auntie that the same thing would happen to her, that is, that she too, there was no knowing why, would close her eyes, stretch out her paws, open her mouth, and everyone would look at her with horror. Apparently the same reflections were passing through the brain of Fyodor Timofeyitch. Never before had the old cat been so morose and gloomy.

It began to get light, and the unseen stranger who had so frightened Auntie was no longer in the room. When it was quite daylight, the porter came in, took the gander, and carried him away. And soon afterwards the old woman came in and took away the trough.

Auntie went into the drawing-room and looked behind the cupboard: her master had not eaten the chicken bone, it was lying in its place among the dust and spiders' webs. But Auntie felt sad and dreary and wanted to cry. She did not even sniff at the bone, but went under the sofa, sat down there, and began softly whining in a thin voice.

VII.

An Unsuccessful Début

One fine evening the master came into the room with the dirty wallpaper, and, rubbing his hands, said:

"Well. . . ."

He meant to say something more, but went away without saying it. Auntie, who during her lessons had thoroughly studied his face and intonations, divined that he was agitated, anxious and, she fancied, angry. Soon afterwards he came back and said:

"Today I shall take with me Auntie and Fyodor Timofeyitch. Today, Auntie, you will take the place of poor Ivan Ivanitch in the 'Egyptian Pyramid.' Goodness knows how it will be! Nothing is ready, nothing has been thoroughly studied, there have been few rehearsals! We shall be disgraced, we shall come to grief!"

Then he went out again, and a minute later, came back in his fur-coat and top hat. Going up to the cat he took him by the forepaws and put him inside the front of his coat, while Fyodor Timofeyitch appeared completely unconcerned, and did not even trouble to open his eyes. To him it was apparently a matter of absolute indifference whether he remained lying down, or were lifted up by his paws, whether he rested on his mattress or under his master's fur-coat.

"Come along, Auntie," said her master.

Wagging her tail, and understanding nothing, Auntie followed him. A minute later she was sitting in a sledge by her master's feet and heard him, shrinking with cold and anxiety, mutter to himself:

"We shall be disgraced! We shall come to grief!"

The sledge stopped at a big strange-looking house, like a soup-ladle turned upside down. The long entrance to this house, with its three glass doors, was lighted up with a dozen brilliant lamps. The doors opened with a resounding noise and, like jaws, swallowed up the people who were moving to and fro at the entrance. There were a great many people, horses, too, often ran up to the entrance, but no dogs were to be seen.

The master took Auntie in his arms and thrust her in his coat, where Fyodor Timofeyitch already was. It was dark and stuffy there, but warm. For an instant two green sparks flashed at her; it was the cat, who opened his eyes on being disturbed by his neighbour's cold rough paws. Auntie licked his ear, and, trying to settle herself as comfortably as possible, moved uneasily, crushed him under her cold paws, and casually poked her head out from under the coat, but at once growled angrily, and tucked it in again. It seemed to her that she had seen a huge, badly lighted room, full of monsters; from behind screens and gratings, which stretched on both sides of the room, horrible faces looked out: faces of horses with horns, with long ears, and one fat, huge countenance with a tail instead of a nose, and two long gnawed bones sticking out of his mouth.

The cat mewed huskily under Auntie's paws, but at that moment the coat was flung open, the master said, "Hop!" and Fyodor Timofeyitch and Auntie jumped to the floor. They were now in a little room with grey plank walls; there was no other furniture in it but a little table with a looking-glass on it, a stool, and some rags hung about the corners, and instead of a lamp or candles, there was a bright fan-shaped light attached to a little pipe fixed in the wall. Fyodor Timofeyitch licked his coat which had been ruffled by Auntie, went under the stool, and lay down. Their master, still agitated and rubbing his hands, began undressing. . . . He undressed as he usually did at home when he was preparing to get under the rug, that is, took off everything but his underlinen, then he sat down on the stool, and, looking in the looking-glass, began playing the most surprising tricks with himself. . . . First of all he put on his head a wig, with a parting and with two tufts of hair standing up like horns, then he smeared his face thickly with something white, and over the white colour painted his eyebrows, his moustaches, and red on his cheeks. His antics did not end with that. After smearing his face and neck, he began putting himself into an extraordinary and incongruous costume, such as Auntie had never seen before, either in houses or in the street. Imagine very full trousers, made of chintz covered with big flowers, such as is used in working-class houses for curtains and covering furniture, trousers which buttoned up just under his armpits. One trouser leg was made of brown chintz, the other of bright yellow. Almost lost in these, he then put on a short chintz jacket, with a big scalloped collar, and a gold star on the back, stockings of different colours, and green slippers.

Everything seemed going round before Auntie's eyes and in her soul. The white-faced, sack-like figure smelt like her master, its voice, too, was the familiar master's voice, but there were moments when Auntie was tortured by doubts, and then she was ready to run away from the parti-coloured figure and to bark. The new place, the fan-shaped light, the smell, the transformation that had taken place in her master—all this aroused in her a vague dread and a foreboding that she would certainly meet with some horror such as the big face with the tail instead of a nose. And then, somewhere through the wall, some hateful band was playing, and from time to time she heard an incomprehensible roar. Only one thing reassured her -- that was the imperturbability of Fyodor Timofeyitch. He dozed with the utmost tranquillity under the stool, and did not open his eyes even when it was moved.

A man in a dress coat and a white waistcoat peeped into the little room and said:

"Miss Arabella has just gone on. After her—you."

Their master made no answer. He drew a small box from under the table, sat down, and waited. From his lips and his hands it could be seen that he was agitated, and Auntie could hear how his breathing came in gasps.

"Monsieur George, come on!" someone shouted behind the door. Their master got up and crossed himself three times, then took the cat from under the stool and put him in the box.

"Come, Auntie," he said softly.

Auntie, who could make nothing out of it, went up to his hands, he kissed her on the head, and put her beside Fyodor Timofeyitch. Then followed darkness. . . . Auntie trampled on the cat, scratched at the walls of the box, and was so frightened that she could not utter a sound, while the box swayed and quivered, as though it were on the waves. . . .

"Here we are again!" her master shouted aloud: "here we are again!"

Auntie felt that after that shout the box struck against something hard and left off swaying. There was a loud deep roar, someone was being slapped, and that someone, probably the monster with the tail instead of a nose, roared and laughed so loud that the locks of the box trembled. In response to the roar, there came a shrill, squeaky laugh from her master, such as he never laughed at home.

"Ha!" he shouted, trying to shout above the roar. "Honoured friends! I have only just come from the station! My granny's kicked the bucket and left me a fortune! There is something very heavy in the box, it must be gold, ha! ha! I bet there's a million here! We'll open it and look. . . ."

The lock of the box clicked. The bright light dazzled Auntie's eyes, she jumped out of the box, and, deafened by the roar, ran quickly round her master, and broke into a shrill bark.

"Ha!" exclaimed her master. "Uncle Fyodor Timofeyitch! Beloved Aunt, dear relations! The devil take you!"

He fell on his stomach on the sand, seized the cat and Auntie, and fell to embracing them. While he held Auntie tight in his arms, she glanced round into the world into which fate had brought her and, impressed by its immensity, was for a minute dumbfounded with amazement and delight, then jumped out of her master's arms, and to express the intensity of her emotions, whirled round and round on one spot like a top. This new world was big and full of bright light; wherever she looked, on all sides, from floor to ceiling there were faces, faces, faces, and nothing else.

"Auntie, I beg you to sit down!" shouted her master. Remembering what that meant, Auntie jumped on to a chair, and sat down. She looked at her master. His eyes looked at her gravely and kindly as always, but his face, especially his mouth and teeth, were made grotesque by a broad immovable grin. He laughed, skipped about, twitched his shoulders, and made a show of being very merry in the presence of the thousands of faces. Auntie believed in his merriment, all at once felt all over her that those thousands of faces were looking at her, lifted up her fox-like head, and howled joyously.

"You sit there, Auntie," her master said to her., "while Uncle and I will dance the Kamarinsky."

Fyodor Timofeyitch stood looking about him indifferently, waiting to be made to do something silly. He danced listlessly, carelessly, sullenly, and one could see from his movements, his tail and his ears, that he had a profound contempt for the crowd, the bright light, his master and himself. When he had performed his allotted task, he gave a yawn and sat down.

"Now, Auntie!" said her master, "we'll have first a song, and then a dance, shall we?"

He took a pipe out of his pocket, and began playing. Auntie, who could not endure music, began moving uneasily in her chair and howled. A roar of applause rose from all sides. Her master bowed, and when all was still again, went on playing. . . . Just as he took one very high note, someone high up among the audience uttered a loud exclamation:

"Auntie!" cried a child's voice, "why it's Kashtanka!"

"Kashtanka it is!" declared a cracked drunken tenor. "Kashtanka! Strike me dead, Fedyushka, it is Kashtanka. Kashtanka! here!"

Someone in the gallery gave a whistle, and two voices, one a boy's and one a man's, called loudly: "Kashtanka! Kashtanka!"

Auntie started, and looked where the shouting came from. Two faces, one hairy, drunken and grinning, the other chubby, rosy-cheeked and frightened-looking, dazed her eyes as the bright light had dazed them before. . . . She remembered, fell off the chair, struggled on the sand, then jumped up, and with a delighted yap dashed towards those faces. There was a deafening roar, interspersed with whistles and a shrill childish shout: "Kashtanka! Kashtanka!"

Auntie leaped over the barrier, then across someone's shoulders. She found herself in a box: to get into the next tier she had to leap over a high wall. Auntie jumped, but did not jump high enough, and slipped back down the wall. Then she was passed from hand to hand, licked hands and faces, kept mounting higher and higher, and at last got into the gallery. . . .

Half an hour afterwards, Kashtanka was in the street, following the people who smelt of glue and varnish. Luka Alexandritch staggered and instinctively, taught by experience, tried to keep as far from the gutter as possible.

"In sin my mother bore me," he muttered. "And you, Kashtanka, are a thing of little understanding. Beside a man, you are like a joiner beside a cabinetmaker."

Fedyushka walked beside him, wearing his father's cap. Kashtanka looked at their backs, and it seemed to her that she had been following them for ages, and was glad that there had not been a break for a minute in her life.

She remembered the little room with dirty wallpaper, the gander, Fyodor Timofeyitch, the delicious dinners, the lessons, the circus, but all that seemed to her now like a long, tangled, oppressive dream.

Histories are more full of examples of the fidelity of dogs than of friends.
--- Alexander Pope

"Bone" Appétit

CAT-egories

1. Starters
2. Sides
3. Entrees
4. Desserts
5. Pet Treats

Spitz's Spinach Dip

2 lbs. baby spinach
1 slice bacon, diced
1 oz. pine nuts
1 oz. peeled garlic, minced
1/3 cup white wine
1 cup grape tomatoes, halved
Salt and pepper to taste
6 each 6-inch pita, cut into quarters

Cook the diced bacon over medium heat until crisp.

Add garlic and pine nuts to the pan and sauté until they begin to toast.

Deglaze (moisten & scrape) the pan with white wine and add tomatoes.

Bring to a boil and add spinach, season with salt and pepper to taste.

Serve in a bowl with pitas on the side for dipping.

(Serves 6)

Smelly Cat Caramelized Onion, Pear & Gorgonzola Pizza

1 each 16-inch pizza crust
4 oz. fresh loaf Mozzarella, sliced
1 each ripe pear, stemmed, seeded and sliced thin
2 oz. walnuts, chopped
3 oz. Gorgonzola cheese
2 ½ oz. sweet onions, sliced and sautéed

Preheat oven to 350°.

Place the pizza crust onto a pizza pan or baking sheet and layer the mozzarella cheese, pear, walnuts, onions and gorgonzola cheese.

Bake for 8-10 minute until the cheese is melted.

Slice and serve.

(Serves 4)

"Sit Up 'n Beg" P.B.J. Wings

10 each 8-10 jumbo chicken wings
Shortening
3 oz. smooth peanut butter
1 oz. grape jelly
1 oz. hot sauce

Dipping Sauce

2 oz. smooth peanut butter
2 oz. Jamaica relish
1 oz. hot sauce

Deep fry chicken wings in shortening for 6-8 minutes until golden and crispy.

In a large mixing bowl, blend peanut butter, jelly and hot sauce. Add wings right from the fryer to the bowl with sauce mixture. Heat from the wings will melt the sauce. Toss very well to coat the wings.

In a small bowl, blend peanut butter, Jamaica relish and hot sauce. Microwave for 30 seconds. Mix well and transfer into a clean bowl.

Place dipping sauce in the center of a dinner plate. Arrange wings around dipping sauce and top with any remaining sauce.

Miss Kitty's Chicken, Apple & Brie Quesadillas

8 each 4 oz. chicken breasts
8 oz. butter
4 each onions, sliced
½ tsp. balsamic vinegar
¼ tsp. sugar
¼ tsp. thyme, chopped
¼ tsp. rosemary, chopped
8 each 10-inch or 12-inch flour tortillas
2 Tbsp. butter
4 each Granny Smith apples, cored and sliced
16 oz. Brie

Sauté the chicken breasts in the butter and set aside.

In the same skillet, add oil and cook the onions, vinegar, sugar, thyme, and rosemary over medium heat for approximately 10 minutes or until onions are golden.

Slice the chicken breast and place in tortilla.

Spoon the onion mixture over half of each tortilla; top with apples and cheese.

Fold over. Cook on the griddle over medium heat for 2-3 minutes on each side or until cheese is melted.

(Serves 8)

Toto's Mallorca Tapas

4 slices of sourdough baguette
1 fresh tomato, peeled and cored
4 slices Prosciutto Ham
Olive oil for drizzling
Salt and pepper to taste

Lightly toast the sourdough slices. Dice the fresh tomato and season with salt, pepper and olive oil to taste. Spread tomato onto the sliced baguette and place prosciutto on top.

Serves 2

Rin Tin Tin's Roasted Beets with
Walnut Tarragon Vinaigrette Salad

1 ½ lbs. beets, red and yellow
4 oz. walnuts, roasted
3 oz. red onion, sliced thin
6 oz. baby spinach
3 oz. spring mix
24 oz. balsamic vinaigrette dressing

Roast the beets, wrapped in foil, at 375° for 1 hour or until the beets can be easily pierced with a fork.

Chill beets; peel and quarter.

Toss the beets, walnuts and red onions with the vinaigrette and serve over a bed of the spinach and spring mix.

(Serves 6)

Calico Cock-A-Leeky Soup

3 medium leeks
1 cup chopped celery
¾ cup chopped onion
3 Tbsp. butter
4 cups peeled and diced potatoes
2 quarts chicken broth
1 tsp. dried rosemary
2 tsp. salt
2 cups whipping cream
3 Tbsp. chopped parsley

Discard roots and tough outer leaves from leeks. Wash thoroughly; chop coarsely. Sauté with celery, onion, and butter in a large Dutch oven until tender (about 10 minutes).

Stir in potatoes, chicken broth, rosemary, and salt.

Cover and bring to a boil. Reduce heat to low; cook 20 minutes.

Stir in whipping cream. Return to serving temperature, but do not boil.

Serve garnished with parsley.

Yield: 3 quarts

<u>Hot Diggity "Cobb" Gourmet Dog</u>

Garnish your favorite dog or sausage with chopped iceberg lettuce and tomatoes, crumbled bacon, and blue cheese dressing!

<u>Hush Puppies</u>

1 cup cornmeal
½ tsp double-acting baking powder
½ tsp salt
2 Tbsp onion, minced
1 egg
¼ cup milk
Vegetable oil

Mix cornmeal, baking powder, salt, and onion.

Beat egg and milk together; combine with dry ingredients.

Form dough into round balls. Deep fry in oil at 370° until golden brown.

Drain on paper towels. (Should be served at once.)

Makes about 12.

Cheshire Cat Cheese Loaf

8 oz self-rising flour
½ level tsp. dry mustard
Pinch cayenne pepper
½ tsp. onion or celery salt
2 oz. butter
4 oz. cheddar, grated
1 beaten egg, combined with ¼ pint milk

Lightly grease a 2-lb loaf tin.

Sift flour, mustard, cayenne, onion or celery salt into a bowl.

Add butter; rub in until mixture resembles fine breadcrumbs.

Stir in grated cheese. Mix with beaten egg and milk to a firm dough.

Turn dough onto a lightly floured board and knead gently until smooth. Form the dough into a roll to fit the prepared loaf tin. Place dough in tin and push out to fit evenly.

Bake in the oven center at 375° for 35-45 minutes, til golden and loaf sounds hollow when tapped.

Cool on wire rack. Slice and serve (best eaten on the day it is made.)

Boston Terrier Baked Beans

1 lb dried navy beans
2 quarts water
1 tsp. salt
1/3 cup firmly packed brown sugar
¼ cup molasses
2 large onions, thinly sliced
4 slices bacon, cut into 1" pieces
1 tsp. celery salt
1 tsp. dry mustard
½ tsp. pepper

Wash beans; place in large Dutch oven. Cover with 2 qts. water. Bring to boil. Cover, reduce heat, simmer 2 minutes. Remove from heat; let stand 1 hour.

Add salt to beans. Bring to boil; cover, reduce heat, simmer 1 hour. Drain; reserve 1 ½ cups liquid. Set aside.

Combine reserved liquid, brown sugar, molasses, celery salt, dry mustard, pepper. Set aside.

Layer ½ of beans, onion, bacon, molasses mixture in 2-3qt. casserole; repeat layers. Cover and bake at 300° for 3-3 ½ hours.

(serves 8)

Tipsy Tabby Asparagus

2 lb. fresh asparagus
¼ cup melted butter
¼ cup white wine
½ tsp. salt
¼ tsp. pepper
1/3 cup grated Parmesan cheese

Snap off ends of asparagus; remove scales with vegetable peeler.

Cook asparagus in boiling salted water until crisp-tender (about 10 minutes).

Place in greased, shallow casserole dish.

Combine butter and wine; pour over asparagus. Sprinkle with salt, pepper, cheese.

Bake at 425° for 15 minutes.

(Serves 6)

Fido Fingerling Potatoes with Wild Mushrooms

4 oz. extra virgin olive oil
2 lbs. Fingerling Potatoes, halved lengthwise
5 Tbsp. shallots, minced
2 garlic cloves, minced
1 lb. fresh wild mushrooms, sliced
Salt and pepper to taste

Toss the potatoes with half of the olive oil.

Place onto a baking sheet and sprinkle with salt and pepper. Roast in a 450° oven for 10 minutes.

Sprinkle with the shallots and garlic and cook until tender.

Sauté the mushrooms in the remaining olive oil until tender. Season with salt and pepper.

Remove the potatoes from the oven and toss with the mushrooms.

(Serves 6)

Bastet's Broccoli Baklava

3 lbs. frozen vegetable mix, stew cut
1 lb. frozen broccoli, chopped
2 cloves garlic, minced
1 box phyllo dough
1 egg, beaten
½ lb. butter, melted
½ oz. sesame seeds
Ground ginger
Salt and pepper to taste

Preheat oven to 350°.

Place stew cut vegetables in food-processor and chop into a barley-sized mixture.

Sauté the first 3 ingredients in the butter until tender, season and cool.

Lay out phyllo dough on the bottom of an oiled cookie sheet and brush butter on the dough with a pastry brush. Repeat this 3 times to have 3 layers of dough sheets.

Spread half of the sautéed vegetables evening over the dough sheets and repeat to end up with 2 layers of vegetables and 3 layers of dough. The top layer will be dough.

DO NOT brush the top layer with butter. Brush the egg on the top layer of phyllo dough and sprinkle sesame seeds on it. Bake in the oven until done.

(Serves 12)

Old Yeller's Chipotle Creamed Corn

2 cups frozen corn
¼ cup red onions, minced
2 each chipotle peppers, chopped
1 Tbsp. chili powder
2 tsp. cumin
1 cup heavy cream
3 Tbsp. unsalted butter
Salt and pepper to taste

Sauté onions in butter until translucent.

Add frozen corn and cook until caramelized (slightly browned).

Add the remaining ingredients and reduce until thickened, approximately 10 minutes.

(Serves 6)

Malamute Mussels Lyonnaise

12 fresh mussels, scrubbed and beards removed
1 stalk celery, shredded
1 small shallot, shredded
¼ cup dry white wine
½ cup heavy cream
3 slices lemon
1 tsp. fresh thyme
1 tsp. Worcestershire sauce
Fresh chopped parsley
Salt and pepper to taste

Place the mussels, wine, shallots, celery, and the lemon slices into a sauté pan. Bring to a boil, and reduce the wine by half.

Add the cream, thyme, and Worcestershire sauce, bring to a boil, then simmer until all the mussels have opened.

Adjust the seasoning with salt and pepper.

Pour into a bowl, and garnish with chopped parsley.

Corgi Coconut-Crusted Lamb Lollipops

24 each single bone lamb chops
1 yellow onion, diced
2 Garlic cloves, crushed
2 tsp. ground turmeric
¼ cup brown sugar
½ cup coconut flakes
2 tsp. soy sauce
2 Tbsp. lemon juice

Trim meat of excess fat, combine all ingredients in bowl, and stir until the coconut is thoroughly moistened.

Add lamb chops and press the coconut mixture onto each one until well coated.

Cover with plastic wrap and marinate for 2 hours.

Preheat grill.

Grill the lamb 2-4 minutes per side or until crisp and golden brown.

Serve immediately.

(Serves 24)

Rover's Rigatoni

3 cups milk
1 Tbsp. carrot, chopped
1 Tbsp. celery, chopped
1 Tbsp. onion, chopped
1 Tbsp. parsley sprigs
¼ tsp. black peppercorns
¼ tsp. hot pepper sauce
½ bay leaf
Dash nutmeg
¼ cup butter
¼ cup flour
1 ½ oz. Parmesan cheese, grated
¾ oz. Romano cheese, grated
12 oz. rigatoni pasta, cooked and drained
6 oz. shredded Cheddar cheese
6 oz. shredded mozzarella cheese
¼ tsp. chili powder

In a 2-qt. saucepan, combine milk, carrot, celery, onion, parsley, peppercorns, hot pepper sauce, bay leaf and nutmeg. Bring to boil. Reduce heat, simmer 10 minutes. Strain and set aside.

Melt butter in a 2-qt. saucepan over low heat.

Blend in flour. Gradually add reserved milk, cook, stirring constantly, until thickened.

Remove from heat, add Parmesan and Romano cheeses, stirring until blended.

Pour over pasta and toss well.

Combine cheddar and mozzarella cheeses.

In buttered 2-qt casserole, layer ½ of pasta mixture, cheese mixture and remaining pasta mixture.

Sprinkle with chili powder. Bake at 350° for 25 minutes or until hot.

(Serves 6)

You Ain't Nuthin' But a Hound-Dog
Corn Bread-Crusted Pork Chops

1 each 6 oz. bone-in pork chop
4 oz. cornbread mix
1 egg, for wash
Salt and pepper to taste
½ tsp. dried parsley

Mix cornbread mix with salt, pepper and parsley.

Dip pork chop in egg wash and coat with cornbread mix.

Place in 400° oven for 6-8 minutes or until golden brown and cover with apple-horseradish sauce.

Apple-Horseradish Sauce

4 oz. chunky applesauce
½ tsp. horseradish

Mix applesauce and horseradish together and let chill for 1 hour.

(Serves 1)

<u>Siamese Shrimp and Pasta</u>

2 cups sugar snap peas
1 ½ cups red bell pepper strips
1 Tbsp. sesame oil
1 Tbsp. grated fresh ginger
2 garlic cloves, minced
1 lb. shrimp
½ cup chicken broth
1 cup coconut milk
¼ cup soy sauce
1 tsp. grated lime zest
1 Tbsp. lime juice
½ cup sliced scallions
Fettuccini or linguine

Cook pasta. Place peas and pepper in a colander; drain the pasta over the pea mixture.

Heat the sesame oil in large skillet over medium-high heat. Add the ginger, garlic, shrimp.

Sauté 3 minutes until shrimp are bright pink. Remove from skillet.

Add chicken broth to skillet. Add coconut milk, soy sauce, lime zest and juice; bring to a boil. Reduce heat; simmer 5 minutes, until slightly thickened.

Add pasta and shrimp; toss together.

Serve topped with the scallions.

Serves 4

Ay, Chihuahua! Chili

4 large garlic cloves
2 medium onions, quartered
1 cup prepared chili sauce
1 Tbsp. tomato paste
1 small chipotle chili (from can of chipotles in adobo sauce)
2 lbs. lean beef stew meat, cubed (3/4")
1 Tbsp. cumin
1 tsp. salt
3 Tbsp. cooking oil
1 cup beef broth

Position rack in center of oven; preheat to 350°.

Mince garlic and onion finely in blender or food processor. Transfer to a sheet of waxed paper. Blend chili sauce, tomato paste, and chipotle til smooth.

Combine beef and cumin and salt in a plastic bag. Seal, then toss well until meat cubes are evenly seasoned.

Heat ½ Tbsp. oil in 3 qt. stove-to-oven casserole over medium-high heat. Brown meat in batches, adding oil if needed. Transfer to a plate.

Add 1 Tbsp. oil to casserole; add garlic and onions. Cover with waxed paper. Cook over medium heat until soft, approximately 6 minutes.

Return meat to casserole. Add chili sauce mixture and ¾ cup beef broth; stir to combine.

Cover and bake in oven until tender, stirring occasionally, about 1 ½ hours, adding more broth as necessary to keep meat covered.

Serves 6-8

Can be prepared ahead: Cover and refrigerate. Bring to room temperature. Reheat at 350° for 30 minutes.

Grimalkin Grilled Salmon Steaks

2-3 salmon steaks, about ¾" thick
2 Tbsp. melted butter
Parsley, chopped
Salt and pepper
Butter to garnish

Brush the salmon with the melted butter; season with salt and pepper.

Place salmon on a well-greased grill rack; have the grill very hot. Grill each side 6-8 minutes, depending on the thickness of the steaks.

Serve garnished with softened butter mixed with chopped parsley.

Lazy Dog Casserole

2 lbs beef chuck, bite-size pieces
½ cup red wine
1 (10 ½ oz.) can beef consommé
¾ tsp. salt
1/8 tsp. pepper
1 medium onion, sliced
¼ cup flour
¼ cup dry breadcrumbs

Preheat oven to 300°.

Combine in a buttered casserole dish: beef, red wine, beef consommé, salt, pepper, onion.

Mix flour with breadcrumbs; stir into casserole.

Cover; bake approximately 3 hours.

(Can be frozen and baked later.)

<u>French Poodle Dijon Chicken</u>

1 (6-oz) jar marinated artichoke hearts
2 chicken breast halves, skinned and boned
1/8 tsp. salt
1/8 tsp. pepper
1 Tbsp. olive oil
½ cup dry white wine
2 Tbsp. Dijon mustard

Drain artichoke hearts; cut in quarters.

Sprinkle chicken with salt and pepper. Brown in hot oil in skillet over medium-high heat.

Combine wine and mustard; pour over chicken. Add artichokes. Cook, covered, over medium heat 10 minutes.

Serves 2

Kitten Kiffles

1 pkg. dry yeast
2 Tbsp. lukewarm water
1/3 lb. butter
2 egg yolks
2 cups all-purpose flour
½ cup light cream

Dissolve yeast in water. Cream butter until soft; stir in unbeaten egg yolks, yeast, flour, and cream. Mix.

Divide into four parts. Chill in refrigerator at least four hours.

Filling:

½ lb. walnuts
1 egg white
1 Tbsp. sugar
1 Tbsp. cream
1 tsp. vanilla

Grind walnuts fine. Beat egg whites until very stiff. Mix nuts, egg whites, cream, vanilla.

Roll one piece of dough very thin on a board sprinkled with flour and ½ cup powdered sugar. Cut dough into 2 ½" squares. Put 1 tsp. filling on each square; roll up neatly. Repeat with the rest of the dough.

Bake on ungreased baking sheet at 350° for 8-10 minutes.

Sprinkle with powdered sugar while still warm.

(We suggest enjoying with a tall glass of cold milk!)

<u>Great Dane(ish) Pastry</u>

1 cup butter
½ cup sugar
1 cup sour cream
1 egg, separated
3 cups all-purpose flour
1 tsp. baking powder
½ tsp. grated lemon rind
2/3 cup chopped nuts
¼ tsp. cinnamon

Cream butter with ½ cup sugar.

Add sour cream and egg yolk; beat until well blended.

Add flour, baking powder, lemon rind. Mix well. Chill.

Shape dough into 2" crescents. Place on lightly greased cookie sheets.

Beat egg white slightly; brush crescents.

Sprinkle crescents with nuts.

Mix cinnamon and 2 Tbsp. sugar; sprinkle on crescents.

Bake at 350° for 15-18 minutes.

Butter Scotch – Terrier Pie

2 egg yolks
1 ½ cups brown sugar
1/8 tsp. salt
1 ½ cups milk
4 Tbsp. flour
2 Tbsp. butter
1 tsp. vanilla
1 baked pie shell

In a double boiler, *over* hot water, combine: brown sugar, flour, butter, salt. Stir and cook until blended.

Add scalded milk.

Beat egg yolks until light. Pour a little of milk mixture over them; beat well. Return it to double boiler. Stir and cook until yolks slightly thicken.

Beat mixture til cool. Add vanilla.

Pour the mixture into the baked pie shell. Bake at 325° approximately 30 minutes. Serve covered with whipped cream.

Pekingese Pecan Cake with Lemon Ice Cream

Cake:

¼ cup butter
1 ¼ cup and 1 Tbsp. sugar
4 eggs, separated
1 tsp. vanilla
3 Tbsp. milk
¾ cup flour
1 tsp. cinnamon
1 tsp. baking powder
Chopped pecans, as desired

Cream butter and ½ cup sugar together. Add 4 egg yolks, well beaten.

Combine milk and vanilla.

Sift together flour and baking powder.

To the egg yolk mixture, add alternately the milk/vanilla and the flour/baking powder.

Spread mixture in two 8" cake pans lined with waxed paper. Preheat oven to 350°.

Beat until stiff 4 egg whites. Gradually add ¾ cup sugar. Spread this meringue on cake mixture.

Sprinkle with pecans and 1 tsp. cinnamon mixed with 1 Tbsp. sugar.

Bake at 350° for about 25 minutes. Turn out on rack to cook, meringue sides d)wn.

Assemble layers, with meringue on top and bottom. Serve with ice cream.

Lemon Ice Cream:

Microwave vanilla ice cream at 30% power at 10-second intervals, til softened. Stir in 1 Tbsp. grated lemon zest and 1 ½ Tbsp. lemon juice. Spread in shallow baking pan and freeze while making the cake.

Purrrrrr-fect Pralines

2 cups firmly packed brown sugar
1 cup buttermilk
1 tsp. baking soda
1 Tbsp. butter
½ tsp. vanilla
1 cup pecan halves (break any large ones)

Simmer brown sugar, buttermilk, and baking soda in a very large, heavy saucepan over low heat ***without stirring***, until mixture reaches 240° on a candy thermometer – or until a bit of the mixture forms a soft ball when dropped into cold water.

Add butter, vanilla, and pecans. Beat vigorously 1-2 minutes, until mixture begins to thicken (it should be the consistency of thick honey).

Drop from a tablespoon onto baking sheets lined with waxed paper, making each praline 2 ½ - 3" in diameter.

Cool to room temperature. Peel pralines from paper and serve.

Angora Cookies (Lemon Snowballs)

½ cup shortening
2/3 cup sugar
2 tsp. grated lemon zest
1 egg
1 ¾ cups flour
3 Tbsp. lemon juice
1 Tbsp. water
¼ tsp. baking soda
½ tsp. salt
¼ tsp. cream of tartar
½ cup finely chopped walnuts
Confectioner's sugar

Mix thoroughly: shortening, sugar, lemon zest, egg.
Stir in: lemon juice, water, flour.

Sift: baking soda, salt, cream of tartar. Stir into mixture. Stir in walnuts.

Flour hands, form dough into walnut-sized balls.

Place 2" apart on ungreased cookie sheet. Bake at 350° 10-12 minutes. (Cookies will be light brown on bottom but not on top). Remove immediately from sheet and roll in powdered sugar.

Pecan Bark

2 cups chopped pecans
2 Tbsp. butter or margarine
1 dash salt
12 oz. vanilla chips or bark
12 oz. peanut butter chips

In a skillet, toast the pecans in the butter and salt, stirring continuously. Set aside.

In a double boiler over boiling water, melt the chips together, stirring until smooth. Remove from heat and stir in pecans, coating well.

Spread a thin, even layer on a wax-paper lined baking sheet. Freeze for 20 minutes.

Break apart into small serving pieces and store in an airtight container.

Makes 2 lbs.

CAT TREATS

Santa Claws Stocking Stuffer

½ cup canned shrimp (drained)   1 cup whole wheat flour
½ cup canned salmon   2 Tbsp. vegetable oil
¼ cup cooked brown rice   1 egg

Preheat oven to 350°. In a medium bowl, combine the shrimp, salmon, rice. Stir in flour, oil, and egg to make a dough. Roll dough ¼-inch thick; cut with cookie cutter. Place on baking sheet; bake 25 minutes. (Makes 2 dozen)

Cheesy Cat-Nips

½ cup shredded string cheese   1 egg
2 Tbsp. soft margarine   ½ cup flour

Preheat oven to 250°. Mix margarine, cheese, egg. Add flour to form dough. Form into marble-size balls. Bake on an ungreased baking sheet 35 minutes. (Makes 1 dozen)

Chicken Cat-cciatore

¼ cup chicken broth   1/3 cup cornmeal
1 cup shredded cooked chicken   1 Tbsp. soft margarine
¾ cup flour

Preheat oven to 350°. Combine chicken, broth, margarine. Add flour and cornmeal. Knead to make a dough. Roll dough to ¼-inch thick; cut with cookie cutter. Place on ungreased baking sheet; bake 20 minutes. (Makes 1 ½ dozen)

DOG TREATS

Mutt and Potatoes

6 oz. ground beef or chicken
½ cup grated carrots

1 cup instant potato flakes
4 Tbsp. powdered milk

Preheat oven to 350°. Purée meat and carrots in food processor. Mix all ingredients. Roll mixture into small bowls and press to make patties. Bake 15 minutes. Keeps 2 weeks in refrigerator. (Makes 24 patties)

Fruit Pup-Sicles

1 quart fruit juice (not grape)
1 ripe banana, mashed
½ cup plain yogurt

Blend juice with banana; mix in yogurt. Pour into ice cube trays and freeze. Serve 1 at a time.

Peanut Butter Bow-Wows

½ cup water
3 Tbsp. peanut butter
1 ¼ cups whole wheat flour

Preheat oven to 350°. Mix all ingredients thoroughly. Spread dough evenly on baking sheet; cut with cookie cutter. Bake 30 minutes, until lightly browned and crispy. Store in an air-tight container. (Makes 2 dozen)